Making a Killing

Making a Killing

Canada's Arms
Industry

Ernie Regehr

McClelland and Stewart Limited

Copyright © 1975 McClelland and Stewart Limited

All rights reserved

0-7710-7438-7

Published in co-operation with the
Mennonite Central Committee (Canada)

The Canadian Publishers
McClelland and Stewart Limited
25 Hollinger Road, Toronto

Printed and bound in Canada

Contents

Preface

An introduction to the Canadian arms industry is not, in the first instance, an exposé of secret sales of Canadian war goods to questionable foreign customers. The argument advanced in the following pages, that the export of arms is an indefensible pursuit, does not depend upon such exports being clandestine in any way. That there are such transactions in need of public attention may well be true—examples of thorough investigative journalism in this field are confined largely to publications outside the mainstream of Canadian journalism—but the emphasis of the following pages will be to expose what is already exposed.

Canadian arms sales are theoretically part of the public record. To be sure, parts of the record are incomplete and government and industry have both sought, not without success, to restrict the circulation of that record. It is a revealing irony, for example, that Montreal's "Project Anti-War" had to go to the Pentagon in Washington for information about Canada's war business which Canadian officials refused to divulge on the grounds that it was "commercial confidential".

But due partly to the persistence of research groups such as "Project Anti-War" and partly to routine government disclosure, a substantial record of the Canadian war business is available, and this study is an introduction to, though not an exhaustive account of, that record. It is offered in the hope that current public ignorance of this unsavoury facet of Canadian diplomacy and industrial enterprise might thereby begin to be challenged. For it is in a climate of public indifference spawned by ignorance that arms manufacturers and salesmen are free to pursue their spurious ends, unencumbered by conscience and even inclined to believe their own dubious rationales.

1 Exploiting the International Arms Market

What differentiates man radically from all other animals is
this, "Thou shalt not kill." For to say that is to flout the
natural course of events. The animal kills what it needs to;
killing is no problem for it at all. Nature is the power to kill.
Slaughter is the basis for the development of life. But when
he says "Thou shalt not kill," man affirms that he is different
from animals, that he has embarked on a new course—in
short, that he has found himself as a man.

Jacques Ellul

Bankrupt Morality and Contravened Self-Interest

Few of man's activities are as cynical in their disregard for the
injunction "Thou shalt not kill" as is the multi-billion dollar trade
in the weapons and paraphernalia of warfare. Amounts spent now
easily exceed 200 billion dollars annually, and for those who measure opportunity in exploitable markets, the arms business has
come upon due season.

Canada's response has been to seek out a reliable corner on the
market. Steady increases in Canadian exports of war materials, or
"defence products," have become a prominent goal and major
achievement of the federal Department of Industry, Trade and
Commerce, and a substantial portion of federal funding of scientific research and industrial development in Canada—some esti-
mate 50 per cent—promotes the development and perfection of internationally saleable military commodities.

The arms merchants—the term includes both government and
industry officials—argue that while it is a circumstance to be de-
plored it is a fact that the commandment against killing is not one
the state can realistically obey. And in a sense they are right. Who

can deny that for states unilaterally to renounce force as a means of self-preservation and to forego violence as a means of enforcing international order would, in the circumstances, very soon lead to the erosion of state authority and, very likely, the disintegration of even that modicum of international order which the world currently enjoys? The world has come to depend upon violence and the threat of violence for its stability and in the process has made violence necessary.

But what has been made necessary is not necessarily just. Though violence be a necessity in the eyes of men and governments absorbed in the exercise of force and the maintenance of power, it does not follow that violence thereby achieves moral validity. Though man has made of violence a necessity, it still debases his humanity; for it is in the renunciation of violence, as Ellul says, that man finds himself as a man.[1] And the extent to which he resorts to violence is the extent to which he has regressed from humanity into profanity. To submit to the "necessity" of violence is to cease to be as free men inasmuch as such submission constitutes acceptance of limits on man's humanity.

The use of force, whether by individuals or states, therefore, is not a sign of strength but evidence of weakness, and those who make it their business to profit from state violence through the manufacture and sale of military commodities do not strengthen the human condition but trade on its weakness.

And while realism demands the concession that the exercise and threat of force have been used to impose a partial and uncertain stability on this world, it is hardly logical to conclude that the near indiscriminate sale of the instruments of force contributes further to that stability. Balance of power diplomacy is something less than a precise science, but the shifting balances of firepower that are the stock-in-trade of the arms merchant hardly contribute to its effectiveness. Peace researchers have long since established correlations between the outbreak of war and the build-up of arms, so that the precarious peace imposed by force is all the more precarious for the efforts of the arms salesmen. (Canadian arms merchants, of course, argue that Canadian arms exports are carefully screened and controlled and are anything but indiscriminate. But it is a claim of dubious worth. Examples of Canadian defence products ending up in places which embarrass Canadian diplomats—examples of which appear in the following pages—are not uncommon. Furthermore, arms merchants often seek to disclaim moral responsibility for their activities with the argument that they have no control over the ultimate use of their products. To sell an airplane or a truck, officials explain, is to do simply that—the vendor cannot determine or prescribe what purposes the plane or truck will eventually serve.)

And if the arms merchant lacks moral validity, he must be found equally wanting as a servant of Canadian self-interest. Canada, it is argued in the following pages, gains neither diplomatic, nor political, nor long-term economic advantage from the export of arms. Since the Canadian arms industry largely follows American models, with a large number of products being manufactured under United States license, Canada's customers tend also to be United States' customers—placing some very obvious restraints on independent Canadian diplomacy. Shared defence production with the United States has essentially given us a shared defence policy, and the comprehensive integration of Canada's defence industry with that of the United States has made this country economically vulnerable to decisions made in the Pentagon and accordingly impaired independent economic planning in Canada.

It is difficult, however, to fault Canadian arms merchants for lack of drive. Since 1965, Canada has consistently sold abroad more than 300 million dollars worth of military products annually.* Sales reached an all-time high of 441.2 million dollars in 1967 when United States purchases of war materials to prosecute the war in Vietnam were at their frenzied peak, and in 1970 the value of war goods produced in Canada for export amounted to more than 16 dollars for every Canadian. In per capita terms, Canadian arms exports exceed those of the United States. In the late 1960s, American arms exports amounted to an annual average of almost $12.50 per capita ($2,500 million worth sold annually), compared with Canadian exports of about $18 per capita ($380 million annually). In absolute terms, Canada now is tied for sixth place with West Germany among the world's arms merchants— exceeded only by the United States, the Soviet Union, France, the United Kingdom, and Italy.

* Export figures are taken from a Department of Industry, Trade and Commerce table entitled "Value of United States and Overseas Procurement in Canada and Canadian Procurement in United States and Overseas." These figures refer only to products specifically classified as defence products purchased by military agencies. Raw materials and fuels, many of which are used extensively for military purposes, are not included in these totals.

The Sporadic Public Debate

The morality of arms sales has only occasionally become the subject of public debate in Canada. And when exports of military commodities have come under public review at all, criticism has usually centred on the ultimate destination of weapons manufactured here, rather than the basic moral validity of arms production and sales, regardless of who eventually uses the products, or in what way.

In 1956 objections were raised when it was discovered that fifteen Harvard training aircraft built in Canada were being sent to Egypt. In that same year Canada had agreed to sell F-86 Sabre jet aircraft to Israel. The ensuing controversy led to the introduction in the House of Commons on January 31, 1956, of a Progressive Conservative motion of no confidence expressing "strong disapproval of the government's policy of authorizing the shipment of munitions of war to countries (in the Middle East) not within the NATO alliance." The CCF Party supported the motion, adding an amendment to the effect that shipments should not have been authorized without making sure that peace in the area would be guaranteed by the United Nations.[2]

The debate did not question the morality of exporting weapons of war, it simply counselled more discretion in the choice of customers.

Similarly, during the height of direct American involvement in the war in Vietnam, opposition to Canadian arms sales to the United States was raised on the grounds that they drew Canada into complicity in a war that most Canadians, including the prime minister, considered to be immoral, or, at the very least, injudicious. Again, opposition was based upon the recipient of the weapons and not upon their manufacture and sale in the first place.

Opposition expressed in those terms has always been to the advantage of those defending arms exports. During the 1968 campaign, Prime Minister Trudeau found himself in that position and answered his critics in this way:

> You know, one of the things in politics is that it just is not feeling. You can feel that the war in Vietnam is wrong, but if you think that by not selling 30 million dollars worth of arms to the United States, if you think this will slow down the war in Vietnam, you are wrong. It will make you feel better, that is all it will do. But if you are not just trying to put balm on

your consciences, if you are not just trying to pretend that you are good guys, if you have the courage of blockading the United States, if you have the courage of saying we are going to cut off commercial relations with the United States. . . . There are some brave guys who say, "Let us do it." Fine. Look, it happens that the United States does not agree with our foreign policy. It so happens that they do not think we should sell wheat to China, it so happens that the United States thinks that we should not trade with Cuba, so what should they do? They do not agree with our foreign policy, therefore they should blockade us. We should blockade them, we should not trade with them and they should not trade with us. You would have a fine world if every time you did not agree with the policy of a foreign sovereign state you decided to blockade it. We would have to blockade France now, we would have to blockade Great Britain, because I hope you do not agree with what she is doing in South Africa. You would have to blockade the rest of Europe. You would certainly have to blockade China because they are a little bit involved in the war in Vietnam too. You would have pure hands, you would have clean hands, but you would have empty bellies and you would be lying flat on your face and you would have a prostrate economy.

The problem of violence in the 20th Century will not be solved by simple solutions like that. nice irony: see p. 11.

The prime minister did not have to face the basic question of the morality of arms sales because his critics did not raise it. The government was criticized only for allowing Canadian-made goods to be put to what the critics considered spurious purposes. Mr. Trudeau was able to restate the criticisms in terms favourable to his own position: The United States, as he interpreted the argument, was pursuing a foreign policy with which Canadians could not agree and the Canadian government was therefore being asked to disassociate itself from that policy by repealing certain trade arrangements between the two countries. In rebuttal, the prime minister had only to explain, in his best professorial manner, that trade policy was not an appropriate means of indicating displeasure at another country's foreign policy. No one, as he saw it, had challenged him to defend a general policy of dealing in war goods.

That is not to ignore, however, the fact that Mr. Trudeau did not deal with the issue quite as fully as he wanted his audience to believe. The value of sales he quoted should have been about 300 million dollars, rather than 30 million dollars, and to equate opposition to a brutal war, in which torture and napalm had become commonplace, with mere opposition to a country's foreign policy is unworthy of anyone who claims to possess even a minimum of sensitivity. There is a qualitative difference between the two, and to argue convincingly that trade cannot depend upon complete agreement in foreign policy hardly leads to the conclusion that a country's participation in a war must leave trade patterns untouched, particularly when the items traded are the tools of war.

Mr. Trudeau's predecessor, the late Lester B. Pearson, also faced a public accounting of sorts for his government's policy of selling war goods to the United States. It was during Mr. Pearson's term as prime minister that the war in Vietnam escalated most dramatically and that Canadian arms sales to the United States followed suit. Mr. Pearson, of course, did much to develop Canada's reputation as a moderate, peace-loving nation and it is interesting, in this light, to see his rationale for continued arms sales to the United States, particularly while the Americans were persisting in a war which Mr. Pearson had publicly criticized. In a letter, dated February 21, 1967, to Prof. Peter Hughes of Victoria College, the University of Toronto, Mr. Pearson stated the government's position in some detail:

Relations between Canada and the U.S.A. in this field are currently covered by the Defence Production Sharing Agreements [sic] of 1959 and 1963, but in fact they go back much farther and find their origins in the Hyde Park Declaration of 1941. During this extended period of co-operation between the two countries, a very close relationship has grown up, not only between the Canadian defence industrial base and its U.S. counterpart, but also between the Canadian and U.S. defence equipment procurement agencies. This relationship is both necessary and logical, not only as part of collective defence, but also in order to meet our own national defence commitments effectively and economically. Equipments required by modern defence forces to meet even limited roles such as peace-keeping are both technically sophisticated and very costly to develop, and because Canada's quantitative needs are generally very small, it is not economical for us to meet our total requirements solely from our own resources. Thus we must take advantage of large scale production in allied countries. As the U.S.A. is the world leader in the advanced technologies involved, and because real advantages can be gained by following common North American design and production standards, the U.S.A. becomes a natural source for much of our defence equipment. The U.S./Canadian production sharing arrangements enable the Canadian government to acquire from the U.S.A. a great deal of the Nation's essential defence equipment at the lowest possible costs, while at the same time permitting us to offset the resulting drain on the economy by reciprocal sales to the U.S.A. Under these agreements, by reason of longer production runs, Canadian industry is able to participate competitively in U.S. research, development, and production programs, and is exempted from the "Buy America" Act for these purposes. From a long-term point of view, another major benefit to Canada is the large contribution which these agreements have made and are continuing to make to Canadian industrial research and development capabilities which in turn are fundamental to the maintenance of an advanced technology in Canada.

In this connection, I should perhaps point out that the greater part of U.S. military procurement in Canada consists, not of weapons in the conventional sense, but rather of electronic equipment, transport aircraft, and various kinds of components and sub-systems. In many cases the Canadian industries which have developed such products to meet U.S. and continental defence requirements have at the same time been able to develop related products with a civil application, or have been able to use the technology so acquired to advance their general capabilities. For a broad range of reasons, therefore, it is clear that the imposition of an embargo on the export of military equipment to the U.S.A., and concomitant termination of the Production Sharing Agreements [sic], would have far reaching consequences which no Canadian government could contemplate with equanimity. It would be interpreted as a notice of withdrawal on our part from continental defence and even from the collective defence arrangements of the Atlantic Alliance.[4]

With his sophisticated and persuasive account of the economic advantages of arms sales, Mr. Pearson offers little in the nature of a moral defence. Defence production sharing with the U.S., he says, helps to maintain "an advanced technology in Canada" and forms the basis of Canadian participation in "continental defence and . . . the collective defence arrangements of the Atlantic Alliance." He does not deny Canadian complicity in the war in Vietnam, neither does the letter deny that an embargo on the export of military equipment to the U.S. would be more consistent with the government's public foreign policy pronouncements against military solutions to political problems. The statement claims only that to impose such an embargo would involve "consequences which no Canadian government could contemplate with equanimity."

Moral ethics are submerged in the language of technological spin-offs and economies of scale.

But economics have not yet become the measure of all things, not even for governments. Their actions are also judged by criteria other than economic viability and, in terms of international diplomacy alone, Canadian arms sales to the United States were, and remain, in the light of the Vietnam war, a travesty of this country's diplomatic honour. Replying to Mr. Pearson's letter, three University of Toronto professors made the simple but incontrovertible point that the sale of war material to the United States "contradicts our disapproval of a military solution (in Vietnam) and discredits our position on the International Control Commission."[5]

T. C. Douglas, then national leader of the New Democratic Party, did not hesitate to refer to the moral issue in opposing the government's position as it was reflected in Mr. Pearson's letter. Mr. Douglas accepted the commitment Canada had made under the Defence Production Sharing arrangements and acknowledged that "we are required to supply weapons for defence." However, he went on to say that the Canadian government should tell the United States that "in our opinion, weapons going to Vietnam are weapons for agression and, unless we can have an assurance that our weapons are not going to Vietnam, we will not sell you arms." He urged the government to follow the example of Sweden in not selling arms until peace comes to Vietnam. Then he stated the moral dilemma as he understood it:

> It is the issue of whether I am prepared to sell a revolver to a man when I suspect he is going to use it to rob some old woman of her life savings. You can always argue that if I

don't sell the revolver, someone else will, or perhaps he will buy a shotgun, which is more dangerous. But this does not relieve me of my moral responsibility. All you can do is live up to your moral responsibility and hope it has some effect.[6]

Mr. Douglas's moral objections to the export of arms depend on the circumstances, but there are those who have objected on the basis of principle rather than circumstance. In March 1970, James Earys wrote:

> To gain influence abroad, full employment at home, the members of the North Atlantic Trafficking Organization are saddling the wretched of the earth with sophisticated weaponry they do not need and can't afford—much as an unscrupulous huckster signs up a family on relief to buy aluminum storm windows or an electric blender. Here is a new form of imperialism—the imperialism of the weapons-pusher. Not even the lambent imagination of a Lenin was able to foresee it.
>
> Is this the foreign policy for a truly just society? There's not much we can do to stop our allies trafficking in arms. But that's no reason to go on pushing the stuff ourselves. If kicking the habit means giving up our membership in NATO, so much the better.
>
> There are two ways of looking at the war business, more decorously called "defence production." One sees it as a national asset which ought to be promoted; the other as a national disgrace which ought to be prevented. Moving from the first to the second of these perspectives is essential to creating that "haven from militarism" which our prime minister has promised to build in Canada—however NATO's fourteen remaining nations may choose to make their living.[7]

The view that has prevailed in the federal government, however, does not see Canada's growing arms export business as a national disgrace. To officials in the Department of Industry, Trade and Commerce it is an economic opportunity, a chance to cash in on the efficiency and economies of scale. By the time of Mr. Pearson's defence of the business, "co-operation" and "specialization" had become the watchwords of the Canadian war industry, following the principle advanced in 1964 by the Department of Defence Production:

> In general, it can be said that unilateral national develop-
> ment of major weapon systems amongst the western coun-
> tries is rapidly giving way to the concept of collaboration
> among allies in defence research, development and produc-
> tion in the interest of conservation of the respective national
> resources in money, manpower and technological capabili-
> ties. In this general direction, with all its inherent difficulties,
> appears to lie the best hope for strengthening scientific and
> technological capability within Canada's engineering indus-
> try.[8]

Instead of each country developing and producing its own full
range of defence equipment, the western allies should pool their
efforts with each country assuming a specialized role. Each of the
countries would specialize in a particular area of development or
production and supply all the others with the results. Costly dupli-
cation of effort would be avoided and the interests of all, individually and collectively, would be served.

The theory may well be defensible for those who are convinced
that an ever-growing and ever-more sophisticated weapons arsenal
is necessary for national and international well-being. But the
theory is badly dented when it becomes clear that the western
industrial allies joined in this co-operative venture in war production do not only supply each other but send their wares literally
around the globe, omitting only those areas that post-World War II
diplomatic tradition has placed on the far side of Winston Church-
ill's iron curtain. Indeed, sales promotional efforts are often concentrated on those very countries referred to by James Earys, those
that neither need nor can afford the military gadgetry concocted in
the laboratories of the affluent.

A list of customers of Canadian armaments includes, among
many others, Botswana, Brazil, Singapore, Zambia, Argentina,
Columbia, Ecuador, Greece, Muscat and Oman, Panama, and
Peru.[9] We can be sure that Canada has no intention of reciprocat-
ing the military purchases of these countries, or of collaborating
with them on the production of sophisticated weapons systems.

Canadian arms sales to countries such as these do not even have
the dubious motive of balancing power in some, by now only
imagined, Cold War. And, in as much as hegemony and industrial
enterprise constitute the only other major motives for the export of
military commodities, Canada is obviously moved most by the

latter. Friends and influence abroad are not shunned as a matter of principle, but hegemony is hardly a realistic aspiration for this country. Furthermore, Canadian arms sales abroad reveal no over-all political design. With the exception of regular sales to traditional allies and restrictions on sales to certain "sensitive" areas, Canadian military products are sold simply to the highest bidder. The motive is profit, purely and simply. How did it come to that? How did it happen that the Canada we thought was so peace-loving—even, we were led to believe until recently, an expert in peace-keeping—turned out to be a major arms merchant, a gun-runner?

Notes

[1] Prof. Jacques Ellul exposes at some length the basis for seeing violence both as "necessity" and human debasement in his book, *Violence: Reflections from a Christian Perspective* (New York: The Seabury Press, 1969), from which the introductory quotation is taken.

[2] This incident and the general question of arms exports are discussed in the booklet, *Merchant of Death?*, by Robert W. Reford (the October 1968 issue of *Behind the Headlines*, published by the Canadian Institute of International Affairs.)

[3] From a speech in Winnipeg, May 23, 1968.

[4] From a letter to Prof. Peter Hughes of Victoria College, The University of Toronto, dated February 21, 1967.

[5] *Globe and Mail*, March 10, 1967.

[6] Quoted by Reford, *op. cit.*, p. 2.

[7] James Earys, *Greenpeace and Her Enemies*, p. 254.

[8] "Defence Expenditure and its Influence on the Canadian Economy," The Department of Defence Production (April 1964) in a House of Commons publication of *Special Studies Prepared for the Special Committee of the House of Commons on Matters Relating to Defence*, p. 104.

[9] *House of Commons Debates*, September 30, 1974.

2 Promoting an Arms Industry

The Canadian Manufacturers' Association sent a delegation
to Britain, not long before the outbreak of W. W. II, in the
hope of gaining for its members a share in the profits of
British rearmament. People so situated were bound to see
war as an economic opportunity.

C. P. Stacey

Re-armament and the Search for Assured Supply

When the Liberal government of Mackenzie King embarked
upon a rearmament program in the late 1930s, it had virtually
nothing to work with. Supplies of equipment and munitions were
at an all-time low and the country possessed, in the words of Colo-
nel C. P. Stacey, formerly the Canadian Army's official historian,
"hardly the rudiments of a munitions industry," let alone the
means to produce extensive military equipment.[1]

It was a state of affairs considered to be rather serious from the
point of view of military planners,* owing to the sharp retreat to
isolationism which followed the experience of World War I. Following that war, in which the Borden government had sent
400,000 Canadian men to the battlefields of Europe, over 60,000
of them to their deaths, "Canadians turned away from Europe
leaving behind their dead."[2] Canada was anxious to affirm North

---

* The then Chief of Staff, Major General A. G. L. McNaughton, reflected
military opinion when he wrote a memorandum to the prime minister, warning that "the situation . . . with respect to equipment and ammunition is one
that can be viewed only with the gravest concern." (Quoted by James Earys
in "Canadian Defence Policies Since 1867," a special study prepared for a
special Commons committee on defence, p. 11.)

America's isolation from the turmoils of Europe and military preparations seemed singularly unnecessary to a small nation that had just sent thousands of her young men to die in a war that, it was already clear, had resolved nothing.

Canadian forces served no military function between the two wars and were, from a military strategist's point of view, sorely neglected. As Canada entered the mid-1930s, however, thoughts again turned to rearmament. While this change in Canadian policy coincided with the remilitarization of Europe, the two were not directly related. Mackenzie King had toured European capitals, including a visit with Hitler, and returned convinced that Germany harboured no aggressive intentions. "Of this I am certain," he told the Canadian people, "that neither the governments nor the peoples of any of the countries I have visited desire war, or view the possibility of war between each other, as other than likely to end in self-destruction, and the destruction of European civilization itself."[3]

Mr. King's assessment of the mood in Europe might have been more credible had it not been for the earlier rearmament efforts of Canada's allies. The 1921 accord between the United States, Britain, Japan, and France, had committed the four powers to a proportional limitation of arms in accord with the *status quo* at that time. Had this agreement actually met the spirit of the Treaty of Versailles' promise of disarmament, much of the appeal of the German Nazis in the early 1930s would have been undermined. While German disarmament was rigidly enforced, the allies' promise of disarmament was not fulfilled. In 1931, Brunning pleaded that if he could offer Germany a genuine pledge of Allied disarmament he could overcome the Nazis; he was made to face the German people empty-handed. When Hitler followed he still claimed that he sought only equality in the matter of armaments—to be achieved either by universal disarmament, which he would accept, or by the rearmament of Germany.[4]

But the Allies chose rearmament—one can only speculate at the consequences had they chosen to disarm—and Canada followed suit; although it is to the everlasting credit of Canadian diplomatic irrelevancy that Canadian rearmament had little to do with power balances in Europe. For Canada, rearmament was more a response to the neglected condition of the armed forces, irrespective of any suspicion that such armaments would actually be employed in the forseeable future, and the equally sorry state of the Canadian economy. Gideon Rosenbluth, in his study of *The Canadian Economy and Disarmament*, points out that "since the beginning of the thirties, depression has been characteristic of periods with no significant military expenditure, while periods with heavy military expenditure have been prosperous. There were only a few exceptional years, in the late 1940s, when both unemployment and defence expenditures were very low."[5] One may be safe in assuming that Mr. King and his associates were not unaware of the economic fallout that would accompany the rearmament program.

But, having decided to rearm fairly extensively and to develop what military planners like to call "a munitions-supply capability," the government had to decide whether these new products, munitions, and equipment would be produced by private industry or in government factories. Mr. King was reluctant to spend the rather large amount required to establish publicly-owned plants, but he was equally dubious about the role of private industry, which was then being investigated in the United States for what were alleged to be unduly large profits and influence. The problem was referred to an interdepartmental committee of civil servants which opted for a privately-owned arms industry, with government involvement to the extent that it would set up necessary machinery to control profits.

Profit control, the main condition under which private industry was to be allowed to produce Canadian defence materials, did not work very well. A year after the committee on profit control had been established, another Royal Commission was established to investigate the granting, without competing bids, of a contract for Bren guns to John Inglis Company of Toronto.

As a result, the government then established a Defence Purchasing Board which was instructed to follow the principle of having, as far as possible, all equipment and munitions for Canadian forces produced in Canada, a principle, it should be noted, that is completely reversed in Lester Pearson's letter of February 21, 1967, referred to earlier. The emphasis in King's time was still on an assured supply, rather than economic advantage, and the King government was willing to pay the price of forgoing the economies of scale. Economic efficiency was to be pursued through competitive bids and, where these were impossible, the restriction of profit to 5 per cent per annum of the average amount of capital employed in the performance of the contract.

By the beginning of World War II, there was still no significant defence industry in Canada,* a condition that was generally blamed on the profit control measures and which led Col. Stacey to conclude that, "both from the point of view of the government's desire to avoid scandals, and from that of efficiency in equipping forces, it is pretty evident that a policy of government manufacture would have had much to recommend it."[6]

With the outbreak of war, Canada still depended heavily on Great Britain for armaments, but when Britain's own needs impaired her ability to supply Canada, efforts were made to purchase supplies from the United States. At that time, however, there were a great many impediments to Canadian equipment purchases in the United States, not the least of which was the fact that in any European war, Canadian forces would be integrated into British field forces, making American-styled equipment a distinct disadvantage.

The Americans themselves were not very keen—much of their defence equipment being produced in government arsenals—and had given little encouragement to a Canadian mission to Washington in April 1938 seeking access to their production.

Unable, at the beginning of the war at least, to purchase any major equipment from the United States, Canada found that not only would she have to supply her own forces but would have to put out a major effort to supply Britain; there should be no surprise in discovering that there were those who saw great opportunity in this. Indeed, it is ironic that it was not until the actual outbreak of war that Canadians began to speak overtly of not only the military necessity but the economic opportunity of rearmament. In

* One Canadian defence industry that did expand extensively in the five years before the war was the aircraft industry. The R C A F was given priority over other services by the King government in its rearmament plan and while most of the new planes were ordered from Britain, some Canadian firms were given smaller orders for the express purpose of encouraging aircraft production in Canada. Production before the war, however, was limited to airframes —that is, airplanes without engines.

Stacey reports that "in 1933 no aircraft were produced in Canada; in 1934 there were 18, and the 'selling value at works' was just $117,689. Thereafter the number rose steadily to 282 aircraft in 1938, with a selling value of $4,001,622; the last twelve months had seen the main increase. The capital employed had still been only $2,836,836 in 1937; the following year it was up to $8,641,790. Though the expansion was impressive, the industry was still small; and the fact that it was entirely dependent on imported engines must be remembered." (Stacey, *op. cit.*, pp. 105-6.)

Mackenzie King's pre-war rearmament program, the over-riding motive for establishing, or at least encouraging, a defence industry, was the assumed need to re-equip and refurbish Canada's fighting forces. The policy of equipping the forces from domestic suppliers undoubtedly had an economic motivation, but security of supply was major consideration. With the outbreak of war, however, another concern arose.

> When the war began, the Canadian economy had not fully recovered from the long world depression, and industrialists were hungry for orders. . . . The Canadian Manufacturers' Association [sent] a delegation to Britain, not long before the outbreak, in the hope of gaining for its members a share in the profits of British rearmament. People so situated were bound to see war as an economic opportunity. And the Canadian government officially took the view that the production of war material would be a primary contribution. . . . [7]

Militarily there were strong reasons why Canadian defence production should be geared to British specifications. In 1909, an Imperial Defence Conference had resulted in an agreement between the United Kingdom and her Dominions to standardize weapons, ammunition, and military equipment, and, in 1939, Canada was still adhering to that policy. The United States was still not in the war, and, as we said earlier, Canadian ground forces were equipped and maintained through British lines of supply and communication.

The job of producing these supplies was obviously a big, and profitable, one. It was brought off largely by the efforts of C. D. Howe, who was put in charge of the new Department of Munitions and Supply, and who set about developing aircraft, naval and land vehicle production facilities, not to mention additional facilities for munitions and a variety of other equipment. At the end of the war, there was little doubt about just how big and profitable the venture had been. Two-thirds of Canadian war production had been sold to foreign governments, according to the following figures reported to the House of Commons:

Destinations of War Materials Produced in Canada[8]

Canada	34%
UK and other	

Empire countries	53%
United States	12%
Other allies	1%
	100%

While there were strong military arguments for integrating Canadian and British defence production systems, as the war progressed and Canadian production increased, other conditions emerged which would gradually drive Canada towards closer cooperation with the United States in defence production. The ultimate entry of the latter into the war was a factor, but more important ones developed before that. Again, the official account is instructive:

> Although Canada made so much material of British types, Canadian industry generally was based upon American production methods, standards and techniques and was dependent upon American imports of machinery, spare parts, subassemblies and components. The production of British-type equipment frequently involved important adaptions of manufacturing procedure to such Canadian-American methods. These industrial problems were paralleled by economic ones which were complicated and in part created by the fact that Canada, alone in the Commonwealth, used dollar currency instead of sterling.[9]

The solution sought and attained by Prime Minister Mackenzie King established the principle which was to lead, almost two decades later, to the Canada-United States Defence Production Sharing arrangements, which, in turn, brought Canada fully into the world of international arms sales.

Canada had almost run out of American dollars by the spring of 1941 and in April Mr. King travelled to Washington to propose "a sort of barter" of war materials between the two countries.[10] His discussions with officials, particularly the then Secretary of the Treasury, Henry Morgenthau, Jr., resulted in the drafting of a set of barter principles. From Washington, King drove to the Hyde Park residence of President Roosevelt to obtain his agreement. A joint statement, later to be known as the Hyde Park Declaration, was issued stating the basic principles upon which King's barter system was to be applied. The statement said, in part:

> It was agreed as a general principle that in mobilizing the resources of this continent each country should provide the other with the defence articles which it is best able to produce, and, above all, produce quickly, and that production programs should be co-ordinated to this end.[11]

The declaration listed a number of commodities which Canada could supply to the United States—munitions, strategic materials, aluminum, and ships—and indicated that Canadian purchases in the United States would include component parts for equipment and munitions which Canada was producing for Great Britain. It expressed the expectation that "during the next twelve months Canada [could] supply the United States with between $200,000,000 and $300,000,000 worth of such defence articles."[12]

Two things, both to have long-term consequences, were formalized in the Hyde Park declaration. First, Canada was actively, albeit under cover of "the war effort," expanding her export trade in arms and, second, the principle was established that Canadian participation in the war industry would henceforth be carried out from a continental, rather than national, base. In later years, the notion of continental defence would logically follow, and that, in turn, would lead to still further integration of the Canadian and American defence industries.

As an arms salesman, Canada was not timid. Following the Hyde Park Declaration, the Department of Munitions and Supply set up a Crown company, War Supplies Limited, "to negotiate and receive orders from departments of the United States government for war supplies to be manufactured in Canada." With that the Canadian government became the formal sales agent for the Canadian defence industry, and it was a role the government was later to refine and expand upon. War Supplies Limited was really a forerunner of today's Canadian Commercial Corporation, the chief difference being that today's arms salesmen have learned discretion in the naming of their agency.

Canadians spared no effort to make War Supplies Limited a successful aid to Canada's unique contribution to the "war effort." According to J. de N. Kennedy's official history of the Department of Munitions and Supply:

> An intensive selling campaign was undertaken by the Company in the United States. Contacts were established with

the senior procurement officers of the War Department, Navy Department, Maritime Commission, Treasury Department, War Shipping Administration, Commodity Credit Corporation, Defence Supplies Corporation, Metals Reserve Corporation, Office of Economic Warfare, also with Washington representatives of the Chinese government, which had large requirements for war materials that could be produced in Canada. The United States government facilitated the selling operations by a series of directives issued to the various procurement agencies and officers.

By the end of July 1941, contracts had been obtained covering approximately $200,000,000.[13]

The Hyde Park Declaration, with its central principle of coordinating military production between the two countries, led to a thorough integration of the defence industries of Canada, the United States, and Britain. In the production of war materials for World War II, borders were ignored, setting a continental pattern from which Canada has yet to extricate itself.

A number of boards and committees were set up to give some formal structure to the integration. A Canada-United States Joint War Production Committee was formed with the specific purpose of integrating the war production of both countries. Officers of War Supplies Limited were prominent on the Committee and through it arranged many of their contracts. Then, on June 19, 1942, the Combined Production and Resources Board was formed, consisting of representatives of the governments of the United States, the United Kingdom, and Canada. The main function of the Board, says Kennedy, was "to combine the production programs of the three countries into a single integrated program adjusted to the stategic requirements of the war."[14] The Minister of Munitions and Supply was the Canadian member on the Board.

A Canada-United States Joint War Aid Committee was also created to co-ordinate the supply of munitions and supplies to allied nations under Canadian Mutual Aid and the United States lend-lease.

The defence industries of the two countries were thoroughly integrated, but that did not, apparently, mean that Canada's industrial contribution to the "war effort" was automatically accepted. Vigilance was the order of the day, and, as Kennedy puts it, "a thorough selling job had to be done to keep Canadian ability to manu-facture war supplies before the United States procurement agen-cies."[15]

From War Effort to Industrial Enterprise

Immediately after World War II, formal measures were taken to continue the "co-operation" which had resulted from the Hyde Park Declaration, but the main concern of the Canadian govern-ment at that time was to dismantle the large military establish-ment, and accompanying arms industry, that had been developed during the war. That spirit of disarmament, however, was soon to be undermined by the West's reaction to the assumed threat of Communist expansion, but it was the Korean War that was most directly responsible for setting official minds towards rearmament once more.[16]

In an exchange of notes between Canada and the United States on October 26, 1950, the principles of the Hyde Park Declaration were reaffirmed and extended to include an agreement that "the economic efforts of the two countries be co-ordinated for the com-mon defence and that the production and resources of both coun-tries be used for the best combined results."[17] The agreement made it clear that Canada had come to view its own defence as a continental, rather than national, matter.

A logical extension of the 1950 principles would later lead to the North Atlantic Air Defence Agreement (NORAD) and the De-fence Production Sharing arrangements,* and it is worth reviewing those principles in great detail:

> 1. In order to achieve an optimum production of goods essential for the common defence, the two countries shall develop a co-ordinated program of requirements, produc-tion, and procurement.
>
> 2. To this end, the two countries shall, as it becomes nec-essary, institute co-ordinated controls over the distribution of scarce raw materials and supplies.

---

* Prime Minister Pearson emphasized the relationship between the Canada-United States arms trade and NORAD when he said, in the February 21, 1967 letter quoted earlier, that the termination of such trade "would be inter-preted as a notice of withdrawal on our part from continental defence and even from the collective defence arrangements of the Atlantic Alliance."

3. Such United States and Canadian emergency controls shall be mutually consistent in their objectives, and shall be so designed and administered as to achieve comparable effects in each country. To the extent possible, there shall be consultation to this and prior to the institution of any system of controls in either country which affects the other.

4. In order to facilitate essential production, the technical knowledge and productive skills involved in such production within both countries shall, when feasible, be freely exchanged.

5. Barriers which impede the flow between Canada and the United States of goods essential for the common defence effort should be removed as far as possible.

6. The two governments, through their appropriate agencies, will consult concerning any financial or foreign exchange problems which may arise as a result of the implementation of this agreement.[18]

The agreement, although simply a statement of principles contained in an exchange of diplomatic notes, is remarkably comprehensive, and includes all essential ingredients for a common market in war materials. There are even provisions for continental controls over the distribution of "scarce" raw materials, and only commitments to share technical knowledge, for example, are left deliberately vague. The United States, with superiority in technological knowledge, obviously meant to decide when exchanges would be "feasible."

Clearly, the basic principles and commitments central to any Defence Sharing Program had been accepted by both countries by the beginning of the 1950s, even though the actual Program was not established until the end of that decade. What remained in 1950 was for events to bring the two governments to the point of publicly and formally establishing the necessary machinery and adopting the pre-requisite domestic policies (such as the elimination of relevant tariffs). And those events were not long in coming.

The main event, of course, was the Cold War, and it, in turn, led to others.

By 1950, the United States was already nervous about the designs of the Soviet Union. The U.S.S.R. had, according to American intelligence, developed both nuclear weapons and the long-range bombers that were capable of dropping them on North

American targets. The American response was to develop a radar system that would warn of any such Soviet bomber attack. Since it was assumed that such an attack would come from the north, over the northern ice-cap, across Canada to destinations in the United States, Canadian co-operation would be required in any radar warning system. And the logical place to install the series of radar stations was the Canadian north. Hence the DEW (Distant Early Warning) Line, Canada's very own Maginot Line. The United States financed and controlled it, while Canadians built it.

The strategic consequences of the DEW Line have long been the subject of debate, but the political consequences for Canada are in no doubt: it brought us NORAD. It has been argued by military strategists that equipment often determines policy;[19] and the DEW Line is a good example. The Americans had spent a great deal of money on the DEW Line and, since it was on Canadian soil, there had to be some kind of joint command. Indeed, as Reford says, the logical step was the establishment of an integrated command for the air defence of North America—hence NORAD, which began operations in 1957.[20]

From NORAD it was not a very long step toward defence production sharing. As Prof. Jon B. McLin put it, "The military integration embodied in the NORAD agreement of 1958 was incomplete if it did not extend to defence production. This judgment was reached by civil servants of the two countries independently of the specific decisions on military equipment that were made in Canada between the spring and fall of 1958. . . ."[21]

The decisions on military equipment which the Canadian government made at the time provided even more impetus to move towards the integration of defence production in the two countries. At issue was the CF-105 Avrow Arrow. The Canadian government had spent a great deal of time and money developing this two-engined, long-range jet capable of supersonic speed, and finally had developed it to the stage, through A. V. Roe Canada Ltd., where full-scale production could begin. For actual production to be economically feasible, there would have to be more planes built than could be used by the RCAF (only 100 by that time) so that, unable to get other orders, the Diefenbaker government announced on February 20, 1959, that the Arrow would not be produced. Gideon Rosenbluth describes the consequences of the decision:

Contract termination caused the loss of hundreds of millions of dollars that had been spent on development, considerable temporary unemployment among certain classes of workers in the Toronto area, and the emigration of a number of scientists and engineers. The reasons given for the termination were that production on the limited scale required by the Canadian armed forces would not be economical, and that it had not proved possible to sell the plane to other countries. The decision that Canada would make no further attempts to develop complete major weapons systems appears to have been made at this time, and has been adhered to by both Conservative and Liberal governments.[22]

These two events, the formation of NORAD and the discontinuation of the Arrow project, were referred to by Raymond O'Hurley, the Minister of Defence Production at the time, as the "two principle developments" which persuaded the Diefenbaker government to enter a Defence Production Sharing arrangement:

The first [development] was the growing integration of Canadian and United States measures for continental air defence, under NORAD, which necessarily involved a greater degree of standardization of defence equipment between the two countries than had been the rule in the past. The other was the increasing complexity of modern weapons systems, which require, in many cases, a range of engineering and production competence beyond the relatively modest resources of this country. . . . [23]

At the same time, Mr. O'Hurley argued that the defence industry which had been built up in Canada over a period of years was considered a "valuable asset," representing "a substantial investment of Canadian resources, a source of livelihood for thousands of Canadian citizens, and a concentration of technical and managerial skills," which the government wanted to maintain and retain in the country. The cancellation of the Arrow production had already heaped a great deal of criticism on the Diefenbaker government, alleging the loss of jobs on a large scale and the exodus of technical skill from the country, and the government now sought to demonstrate that it was in the business of creating jobs.

Moreover, said Mr. O'Hurley:

The development and production of defence equipment has shown a growing tendency to set the pace of industrial progress for a country, and this was certainly true of Canada. Although many of our weapons have no close counterparts in civilian life, most engineering developments for defence needs have found more or less direct and immediate applications in the civilian market.* As long as Canada must maintain a defence program of major proportions, we must ensure that Canadian technology shall enjoy as much as possible of this incidental benefit.[24]

The argument was beginning to shift. The main arguments given in support of a thriving defence industry remained the need to back up Canadian defence equipment procurement, but the defence industry was now being defended for its own sake. During World War II, Canadians argued that a great deal of money was going to be spent on war goods so Canada, as part of its war effort, should make a point of getting in on the market, but now it was being argued that the defence industry was particularly important because it set the pace of technological development, not to mention job creation. A war industry could be a very useful economic tool to which any government would be grateful to have access.

By 1964, while defence production sharing and a domestic defence industry were still being defended primarily on grounds of meeting Canadian defence supply requirements economically and efficiently, the government was citing large exports of defence commodities as one of the major benefits of a defence industry. Here is how it was explained in the White Paper on Defence published in March 1964:

Since the end of the war, weapons and weapons systems have steadily become more complex and costs have mounted rapidly. Only the largest powers can economically design, develop and produce all their weapons. Therefore, there is a

---

* This argument continues to be advanced by defenders of military equipment producers even though it has been thoroughly discredited on numerous occasions. The July 1971 issue of the *Pugwash Newsletter*, for example, stated that the civil "spin-off" from military activity is perhaps 10-20 per cent of the military expenditure—and that it is most unlikely to be more than 20 per cent. If the same resources were applied directly to civil problems, the figure would, of course, be 100 per cent.

need for greater inter-allied co-operation to harmonize defence requirements and to co-ordinate production programs.
Such co-operation was the establishment of the Canada-
United States Defence Development and Production Sharing Program.

Within the past two years efforts have been made to extend this collaboration in defence production beyond the
United States to our NATO allies, and appropriate arrangements have been initiated with Britain, France and a number
of NATO countries.

It is considered that the hundreds of millions of dollars of
foreign orders reaching Canada annually are evidence of
progress made with its allies in production for defence. It is
in the context of these arrangements that it has been possible
to justify the procurement of certain weapons developed and
produced abroad.[25]

The policy of shared defence was most clearly embodied in the
NORAD agreement while the policy of shared defence production
was given its most detailed and explicit formation in the Defence
Production Sharing arrangements made between Canada and the
United States in 1959. The agreement, although there is no signed
agreement, only a set of principles published by the two countries,
outlines specific measures to allow Canadian industry direct access
to the American market for defence products. The Canadians had
argued that shared defence should lead to shared production, and
since American industry had, for some time, been supplying much
of Canada's military requirements, provisions should be made to
allow Canadian industry access to the American market.

The main provisions of the Defence Production Sharing arrangements were published in the November 1959 issue of *Industrial Canada*:

> To promote U.S.-Canadian defence production sharing the
> United States government is:
>
> 1. Waiving regulations of the Buy American Act for
> purchase in Canada of the main kinds of defence equipment
> which Canadian industry is able to produce.
>
> 2. Waiving import duty, in most cases, on products of
> Canadian firms sub-contracting from U.S. prime contrac-
> tors.

3. Relaxing security restrictions to permit freer discussions with U.S. Armed Forces and U.S. defence contractors of many important projects which have legitimate interest for production-sharing Canadian industries.

The Canadian government is:

1. Increasing the staff of the Washington office of the Department of Defence Production.

2. Appointing officers to the principal U.S. procuring centres and contracting areas.

3. Providing, on a continuing basis, detailed, up-to-date reports of Canadian production facilities to U.S. procurement centres and contracting areas.

4. Assisting Canadian firms in making direct contacts with major U.S. contractors in programs lending themselves to production sharing.

5. Successfully encouraging U.S. contractors to visit Canada for a first-hand look at Canadian production facilities.

6. Sifting U.S. procurement programs for opportunities most likely to interest Canadian manufacturers.

7. Underwriting partial cost of pre-production and tooling for Canadian firms in cases where such firms are bidding again U.S. firms whose pre-production and tooling costs have already been written off under previous contracts.

8. Aiding Canadian industries in securing development contracts of an advanced nature, in order to keep Canadian skills abreast of developments in defence technology.

Canadian industry is urged to:

1. Be efficiency—and cost—conscious in manufacturing operations.

2. Use imagination and engineering skill of a high order in framing production sharing proposals.

3. Concentrate Canadian development and production on the things Canadian manufacturing industry can do best.[26]

The guidelines are obviously comprehensive and designed to promote production efficiency and technical skill in supplying the United States military with the equipment it believes it needs to defend North America. They commit the Canadian government to "underwriting partial cost of pre-production and tooling for Canadian firms" to maintain competitive positions with American firms and, significantly, move Canadian industry in the direction of further specialization —Canadians are urged to concentrate on what they "can do best."

But there are some limitations on production sharing. "Off the shelf" general procurement is excluded from the arrangements, as are basic raw materials, fuels, lubricants, and services such as transportation, rentals, and maintenance (consequently, export figures do not include sales of these items to the American defence department, estimated by the Stockholm International Peace Research Institute to exceed $200 million per year). In addition, there are limitations in respect of participation by Canada in the supply of food, clothing, ships, and certain classified products. There are also some special United States provisions relating to small business, depressed industries, and business awarded in labour surplus areas.

A 1970 Commons Committee report describes some of the results of Defence Production Sharing:

> Current relations between Canada and the United States in the field of defence trade are governed mainly by the arrangements agreed upon by the two countries in 1959 and 1963. The total value of United States defence procurement in Canada from the beginning of the Production Sharing program in 1959 to the end of December 1969 has been $2,418.8 million. The corresponding value of Canadian defence procurement in the United States in the same period has been $1,913.8 million.
>
> For the most part, United States military procurement in Canada consists not of armaments or weapons in the conventional sense, but rather items with a high technological content such as transport aircraft, aircraft engine and airframe components, navigation equipment and spares, ammunition components, marine valves and vehicle components.[27]

While the Defence Production Sharing arrangements were obviously based on what the two governments considered to be mutually beneficial factors, the motives of each were really quite different. The United States government was primarily concerned with military security while the Canadian government's concern had come to be centred on industrial development (particularly since Canadian military exports to the United States had fallen from $124 million in 1953 to $43.7 million in 1957). Gideon Rosenbluth points out that in descriptions of these programs, American documents emphasize co-operation and integration of military planning while the Canadian counterparts emphasize the integration of the defence industry and the development of a competent defence industry in Canada[28]—competence being measured by the ability to compete effectively for foreign sales. For the United States, the advantages are assumed to be of a military/security nature while for Canada they are commercial—a difference of emphasis that should hold little comfort for Canadian nationalists. While Canada has sought short-term financial advantage, the United States has sought influence, if not control, over military planning for the continent and the submersion of any national objectives in favour of the so-called continental interest.

A 1960 United States Defence Directive, the basic American defence document dealing with Defence Production Sharing, "stipulates the policy of maximum production and development program integration in support of closely integrated military planning between the United States and Canada."[29] Among the detailed objectives listed by the Directive are "the determination of Canadian production facilities available for the supply of United States current and mobilization requirements, and the furnishing of planned mobilization follow-up schedules to Canadian contractors producing for the United States as guidance in the event of full mobilization."[30] (In 1963, the joint arrangements were extended to include areas of research and development.)

In Canadian policy statements, says Rosenbluth, the emphasis differs from that found in the United States directives. While such words as "collaboration" and "co-ordination" occur, the stress is on the generation of business for Canadian firms, in the context of a situation where major items have to be procured abroad. Thus, while the American statements stress that without production sharing, the Canadian defence industry would not be integrated with that of the United States, the Canadian statements seem to say that without production sharing the Canadian defence industry would not exist on its present scale. "Production sharing is thus, on the Canadian side, an aspect of the general policy of promoting and protecting defence production in Canada."[31]

The main Canadian argument in favour of production sharing in defence commodities clearly is the economic one. In fact, there is little doubt that the sharing of development and production facilities with the United States has maintained and expanded the Canadian defence industry to the point where it is becoming a major exporter and important source of foreign currency. Critics of the program can hardly deny that jobs are created directly because of the export of arms, and indirectly, although to a much lesser degree than claimed, as the result of technological spin-offs from arms production which lead to innovations and new commodities in the civilian consumer market. In some cases, arms exports have also resulted in lower prices for certain civilian goods in Canada. Some industries, the electronics industry for example, can produce products for domestic, non-military use at a loss and then make up that loss by producing military equipment for export, mainly to the United States, at a substantial profit. Ottawa trade officials claim that, in several fields, products are, in fact, being subsidized by military production and that all Canadians benefit.

These benefits are gained at not only high moral cost, but high political and economic cost as well. Political and economic costs are incurred in that defence production sharing programs encourage and facilitate the integration of the defence industry in Canada with that of the United States. The standardization of defence equipment between the two countries is part of that process and, to the extent that defence policy is determined by hardware (and, as we noted earlier, Colin Gray suggests that equipment is a *major* factor in determining defence policy), the defence policies of the two countries tend to become co-ordinated or integrated, or whatever euphemism one may prefer, leaving little doubt about which country determines what the North American defence policy finally will be. And because the United States is the larger of the two and with a larger defence industry, and is undeniably the dominant force in defence policy formulation, the overall weapons systems are developed and produced there. Canadian industry becomes the supplier of specialized component parts. Indeed, as the conditions of the Production Sharing arrangements make clear, it is part of conscious policy to encourage specialization in the Canadian industry. The consequence of specialization is that Canadian industry becomes largely dependent on the American parent industry. The parts produced in Canada are useless without the dominant American weapons system.

This vulnerability of the Canadian industry, this essential dependence on decisions made in the Pentagon, has led Canada to seek alternative markets. If our special component parts of an American weapons system can be sold elsewhere, then a bit more stability and "confidence" can be instilled in the industry. So, defence production makes Canada dependent on the United States and also encourages her to become a major arms exporter in order to reduce that dependence.

That Canada is seeking to expand her export trade in arms beyond the United States is confirmed by government officials. The 1968 "Annual Report of the Department of Trade and Commerce" says, for example:

> During 1968 efforts were continued to establish co-operative defence development and production programs with Canada's NATO partners and other friendly countries. Briefings, missions, and industrial tours were utilized to bring the special technological skills of Canadian defence industry to the attention of those countries as a basis for possible collaborative programs.[32]

Incidentally, it is interesting that just at the time Prime Minister Trudeau and his colleagues, not to mention the public at large, were debating the merits of withdrawing from NATO, Trade and Industry arms salesmen were trying to persuade NATO countries to enter into special arms-production arrangements with Canada. Little wonder the government decided that Canadian interests would best be served by staying in the NATO alliance.

But even in seeking additional markets for defence products overseas, Canadians are, to a significant degree, dependent upon the United States. Because the Canadian industry generally follows American models, Canadian exports must generally be made to other countries that also follow the American model. Hence, America's friends and customers must become Canada's friends and customers, which may explain why we tend to sell military hardware to countries like Brazil, a good customer for Pratt &

Whitney PT6 A-20 aircraft engines, made by United Aircraft in Quebec, for use by the Brazilian air force.[33]

Most Canadian politicians, however, see little danger of dependency in the Canada-United States Production Sharing arrangements. During the second session of the twenty-eighth Parliament (1969-70), the Commons Standing Committee on External Affairs and National Defence reviewed defence production sharing and came to this conclusion:

> The Committee has also concluded that while continuing attention is required, the Defence Production Sharing Program has not, up to the present time, been the cause of undue dependency on the United States, and that on balance the program has operated to Canada's advantage.[34]

Moral outrage at the export of military equipment, as suggested earlier, must include recognition of the economic consequences of cutting off those sales and such outrage cannot logically be confined to military equipment. The United States, for example, could get along without our manufactured military products much more easily than without some of our natural resources, which is why the 1950 principles include joint control over scarce raw materials. Raw materials exported to the United States by Canada, in many instances, go directly into the production of defence goods or in support of the United States military in other ways. Oil and gas are good examples.

Canada supplies over 75 per cent of the gas needs of the Montana Power Company, which, among other things, supplies the massive Montana operation of Anaconda Copper Mining Company, a major supplier of strategic metals. During the Korean War, the company faced a serious shortage of gas when indigenous sources became scarce and when Alberta refused to authorize exports because its own requirements had not yet been adequately assessed. Because of the strategic nature of Anaconda's operation, Alberta's priorities could not be allowed to prevail and one wonders whether the subsequent course of events, as reported in a study of trade in gas and oil by John J. Miller, offers an example of the kind of thing that happens often in an integrated, co-ordinated North American defence production system:

> The Canadian Department of Defence was asked to in-

tercede with the province to ensure that the necessary supplemental gas supplies would be made available. A special law was enacted by the province authorizing the removal of up to 10 bct per year at a daily rate of 40,000 mct, from specified gas fields, for the exclusive benefit of Anaconda Copper Mining Company. A license to export was granted in 1951 by the Minister of Trade and Commerce under the Expropriation of Power and Fluids and Importation of Gas Act, and the Board of Transport Commissioners authorized the necessary pipeline construction in Canada under the Pipeline Act.[35]

Notes

[1] The following account of Canada's entry into extensive private production of war commodities is based substantially on Stacey's study, *Arms, Men and Government: The War Policies of Canada 1939-45* (Ottawa: The Queen's Printer, 1970).

[2] James Earys, *Canadian Defence Policies Since 1867*, p. 7.

[3] Ibid., p. 70.

[4] William Robert Miller, *Nonviolence, A Christian Interpretation* (New York: Schocken Books, 1966).

[5] Gideon Rosenbluth, *The Canadian Economy and Disarmament* (Toronto: Macmillan, 1967), p. 7.

[6] Stacey, *op. cit.*, p. 102.

[7] Ibid., p. 485.

[8] *House of Commons Debates*, November 19, 1945.

[9] Stacey, *op. cit.*, p. 489.

[10] Reford, *op. cit.*, p. 5.

[11] *Industrial Canada*, November 1959.

[12] Ibid.

[13] J. de N. Kennedy, *History of the Department of Munitions and Supply: Canada in the Second World War*, 2 Vols. (Ottawa: King's Printer, 1950), pp. 494-95.

[14] Ibid., p. 476.

[15] Ibid.

[16] Escott Reid, from a speech March 28, 1969; quoted by John Gellua in *Canada in NATO* (Toronto: Ryerson Press, 1970), pp. 19-20.

[17] *Industrial Canada*, November 1959.

[18] Ibid.

[19] Colin Gray, *Canadian Defence Priorities: A Question of Relevance* (Toronto: Clarke Irwin, 1972). Gray refers to this more than once, notably in the Preface pages 1 and 27.

[20] Reford, *op. cit.*, p. 8.

[21] Jon B. McLin, *Canada's Changing Defence Policy 1957-63* (Baltimore: Johns Hopkins Press, 1967), p. 179.

[22] Rosenbluth, *op. cit.*, p. 33.

[23] *Industrial Canada*, November 1959.

[24] Ibid.

[25] "1964 Defence White Paper," p. 28.

[26] *Industrial Canada*, November 1959.

[27] "Eleventh Report of the Standing Committee on External Affairs and National Defence."

[28] Rosenbluth, *op. cit.*, p. 36.

[29] Ibid.

[30] Ibid.

[31] Ibid.

[32] "Annual Report" (1968), Department of Industry, Trade and Commerce (Ottawa: Queen's Printer).

[33] *Foreign Trade*, May 22, 1971.

[34] "Eleventh Report," *op. cit.*

[35] John J. Miller, *Foreign Trade in Gas and Electricity in North America: A Legal and Historical Study.*

3   Marketing the Product

We wouldn't be around here very long if we held very strong
views about what we produce and what its used for.

The President of a Canadian
arms exporting firm.

The Public Servant as Arms Salesman

Free enterprise and Canadian ownership are not hallmarks of
the defence industry. From its humble beginnings with Mackenzie
King's pre-war rearmament program, the Canadian defence industry has been the carefully nurtured child of government. And as for
Canadian ownership, that quickly gave way to the claimed efficiency of vertical integration and continental co-operation—with
the Canadian government following suit with what is euphemisti-
cally called a co-ordinated North American defence policy.

Through it all, the interests of the companies were, and still are,
assumed to be one with that of the country's. It comes as no
surprise, therefore, to learn that the governments that have for the
last three decades claimed that what is good for the defence industry is good for Canada, have also done their part to aid, not to
mention abet, the aspiring arms merchants in very concrete ways.
Not the least of these is sales promotion, and the federal bureauc-
racy boasts an entire division deployed in the worldwide war to
win arms sales. The object is trade, balance of payments, foreign
currency earnings—in short, economics. Military security or strategy or defence plays little part in the Canadian arms export business.

The primary aid given by the federal government to the arms
industry is through the "International Defence Programs Branch."
IDP is a branch of the Department of Industry, Trade and Com-

merce and enlists the efforts of some eighty men and women in facilitating the sale of Canadian-made defence products abroad. The group has two main functions. In the first place, it has representatives stationed at strategic centres around the world to keep track of the defence equipment and weapons needs of foreign armed forces. Representatives in London, Bonn, Brussels (NATO), Rome, and Tehran make it their business to be familiar with the requirements of foreign governments and to pass the information on to the Canadian suppliers. The efforts of these representatives are augmented by a special office in Washington and by trade officers attached to Canadian embassies around the globe.

The second function of the IDP Branch is to assist Canadian suppliers in bidding on defence contracts, in meeting the terms of the Production Sharing Program, and in generally coping with the administrative and diplomatic red tape that is an inevitable part of international defence sales. In short, the branch acts as liaison between Canadian industry and foreign buyers.

In explaining "How to Participate in the Defence Market," a Department publication explains its role in this way:

> To compete successfully in the international defence market, a company requires the managerial, engineering, technical and financial resources to justify a decision to share with government the high risks involved in defence research, development and production. ... The Department through the International Defence Programs Branch will assist companies to receive bid documents, aiding in a search for financial assistance, facilitating appraisals of unsolicited proposals.[1]

Financial assistance comes under a variety of programs. The Department of Industry, Trade and Commerce itself operates a wide variety of industrial assistance programs, and, for the defence industry in particular, the Defence Industry Productivity Program. But before going into more detailed description of the government's direct financial assistance to the defence industry, a few more things can be said about other forms of government aid.

A major form of aid is in helping Canadian companies cut through the masses of red tape that accompany defence contracts. For example, a major problem for American defence contractors purchasing defence products from Canada, according to the Department, is delivery:

> Frequently, critical delivery dates must be met and although a Canadian source may provide a better price, the U.S. buyer may be reluctant to place the order in Canada because of the possibility of delays at the border. The most common cause of delays in shipments is failure to complete shipping invoices and other documents correctly. . . .
>
> A second reason for reluctance on the part of U.S. buyers to place defence orders in Canada is concern about additional administrative procedures that may be required to clear shipments through customs, i.e., the determination if the supplies are eligible for duty-free entry, or the possibility of disputes and difficulties over payment of duty if it is later determined that a shipment was not eligible for duty-free entry.[2]

To overcome these problems, the Department publishes a *Defence Export Shippers' Guide*, a detailed guide to completing various forms and documents which includes tips on how to get through the bureaucratic maze with a minimum of delay. The booklet is a detailed guide and augments the assistance given by departmental personnel to the industry.

There is still another means by which the federal government assists Canadian defence manufacturers in the sale of their wares. The Canadian Commercial Corporation is wholly owned by the Government of Canada, through the Department of Supply and Services, and was established in 1946 to act as the contracting agency when other governments wish to purchase defence or other supplies and services from Canada on a government-to-government basis. Canadian producers can deal directly with foreign governments in defence production, provided an export permit is obtained, but there are obvious advantages in working through the Corporation. As an enthusiastic writer in *Canadian Business* allowed:

> The operations of the Corporation cover a broad spectrum of international transactions. While one officer is negotiating

a contract for the provision of 105 military aircraft for the Netherlands government (as one did in February, 1967), another may be rounding up 75 million vitamin capsules for UNICEF and a third investigating Canadian sources of electrical generating equipment for India or a modern communications system for Thailand.[3]

The Corporation offers the full range of services required to sell products abroad. The manufacturer enters into contract with the Canadian Commercial Corporation to supply goods which the CCC has already contracted to supply to a foreign government. Since the Canadian supplier's contract is with the CCC, that transaction is entirely in Canadian dollars.

When the Corporation receives a request for a quotation from a foreign government, competetive bids, wherever possible, are obtained from Canadian suppliers. The bids are evaluated by the CCC and submitted to the enquiring government, and, if the offer is accepted, the CCC enters into contract with both parties, with identical terms and conditions with the foreign government and the Canadian supplier. In other words, the entire purchasing organization of the government becomes available to the Canadian exporter.

Defence products are the largest commodity group traded under the CCC and the United States government is the largest purchaser, under the Defence Production Sharing arrangements.

An important sales-aid is the 500 page catalogue of *Canadian Defence Products*, published by the Department of Industry, Trade and Commerce (See Appendix I). The catalogue includes an index of companies in the defence business, with brief descriptions of the specialities of each. An index of commodities, with pictures and descriptions, is also included along with information about how to go about buying them.

Government assistance to the Canadian defence industry, in the form of management and sales expertise and liaison with foreign governments, is provided primarily by the Department of Industry, Trade and Commerce (including the International Defence Programs Branch), the Department of Supply and Services (including the Canadian Commercial Corporation), the Department of National Defence, and the Treasury Board. In the fiscal year

1972-1973, these administrative services cost the taxpayer more than $5.5 million.[4]

The cost of direct financial assistance, however, makes rather higher demands on the taxpayer. Grants are made through a variety of programs and the actual extent of the federal government's financial contributions to the post-research stages of the defence industry is not easily ascertained (government support of defence research will be discussed below, even though the distinction between research, development, and production is in many ways artificial).

Of the approximately $100 million which the Department of Industry, Trade and Commerce spends annually on industrial development, about 40 per cent is specifically referred to as being spent "to develop and sustain the technological capability of Canadian defence industry for the purpose of defence export sales or civil export sales arising from that capability." (The 1973-1974 estimates include $43,750,039 in such grants to the defence industry, and in 1972-1973, $48,324,792 was actually spent—see breakdown in Appendix V.)[5] Another 25 per cent is specified to be for non-defence purposes, but the remainder is said to be simply for "general incentives to industry for the expansion of scientific research and development in Canada." Department officials admit that this rather vague category includes both military and civilian research, indicating that at least 50 per cent of these research and development funds are for military purposes.

The Defence Industry Productivity Program is the Program under which the grants specifically in support of defence technology are issued to industry by a) assisting in the development of specific defence products for export; b) the acquisition of modern machine tools and other advanced manufacturing equipment to meet exacting military standards; and c) assistance with preproduction expenses to establish manufacturing sources in Canada for export markets.[6] This Program combines two earlier ones: The Defence Export Development Program, begun in 1964, and the Defence Industries Plant Modernisation Program, started in 1959. Between 1964 and 1968, some 200 projects involving a total expenditure of $165 million were supported, with the government providing about $100 million. The remainder was provided by the firms involved or, in some instances, by other NATO governments. The Department of Industry claimed that the projects generated sales amounting to $924 million. In fact, the program was considered so successful that government funding has more than doubled to current levels of more than $40 million annually.

Other granting programs which may also support companies involved in defence production include: the Industrial Design Assistance Program, Program to Enhance Productivity, Program for the Advancement of Industrial Technology, General Adjustment Assistance Program, Program for Export Market Development, and the Ship Construction Subsidy Program.

During the period 1967-1971, the Department awarded a total of $458,643,906 to 154 defence contractors in Canada. Of these companies, the ownership of 102 was determined, and of these 45 were American-owned. These 45 companies received $224,-492,428, or 47 per cent of the total grants.[7]

An example of the government's growing interest in defence production for export is its rapidly increasing support for defence industry modernization. The program was begun in 1964-1965 with 19 projects at a cost of $474,000. By the next year, it had risen to 40 projects and $2,440,000. A major increase took place the following year, 1966-1967, when 98 projects were funded to the tune of $8,000,000, and in 1967-1968 the program funded 95 projects with $10,581,000.[8]

The Department of Industry, Trade and Commerce sees its many-pronged assistance to Canada's growing defence industry as an effective way of upgrading the technological and production capabilities of Canadian industry. Their job, officials say, is to promote Canada's competitive position in world markets. Military hardware, they reason, constitutes a continuing and expanding market and is a means towards better competition in non-military fields.

Arms and the Economy

The measure of success of the government's assistance to the Canadian defence industry is, of course, to be found in the export performance of the industry,* and there is obvious pride in the faces of

---

* Basically, a defence export is the export of a product that is purchased by a department of defence, but there are some important exclusions. Items not included are: "Off the shelf" general procurement (such as household goods, personal items and food); construction (including installation associated with construction); basic raw materials; fuels and lubricants; and services (such as transportation, rentals and maintenance of fixed installations).

officials of the International Defence Programs Branch when the statistical tables are displayed. Since 1959, when production sharing first began, there has been a consistently high volume of sales to the United States, accompanied by rising sales to other governments, as the following two sets of figures show.[9]

Sales to the United States
(Millions of Canadian Dollars)

1959 —	96.3
1960 —	112.7
1961 —	142.6
1962 —	254.3
1963 —	142.0
1964 —	166.8
1965 —	259.5
1966 —	317.1
1967 —	307.7
1968 —	320.0
1969 —	299.8
1970 —	226.5
1971 —	216.3
1972 —	N/A
1973 —	N/A

The peak years of the Vietnam war were also the peak years for Canadian sales, but even without these extra sales, Canada has had a steady and significant market in the United States.

Sales to other governments are not as high, but the rate of increase is much more dramatic. Since 1950, according to the Stockholm International Peace Research Institute, major Canadian weapon exports to third world countries have averaged $23 million per year.

Sales to Other Countries,
Excluding the United States
(Millions of Canadian Dollars)

1959 —	N/A
1960 —	N/A
1961 —	N/A
1962 —	45.1
1963 –	53.2
1964 —	59.8

```
1965 —   67.7
1966 —   78.3
1967 —  133.5
1968 —  109.2
1969 —  100.1
1970 —  109.7
1971 —  120.0
1972 —  N/A
1973 —  N/A
```

**Total Sales to
All Countries
(Millions of Canadian Dollars)**

```
1959 —  N/A
1960 —  N/A
1961 —  N/A
1962 —  N/A
1963 —  195.2
1964 —  226.6
1965 —  327.2
1966 —  395.4
1967 —  441.2
1968 —  429.2
1969 —  399.9
1970 —  336.2
1971 —  336.3
1972 —  300.4
1973 —  308.2
```

Clearly, these figures confirm the suggestion made earlier that Defence Production Sharing with the United States promotes the export of military commodities to other countries. Indeed, Branch officials claim that for every dollar's worth of sophisticated, high technology defence equipment sold to the United States under Defence Production Sharing, about another fifty cents' worth of the same product is sold to another military. Beyond that, it is claimed that almost another dollar's worth will be sold to the American civilian market as a result of the original sale.

The argument is extended further to say that the development of technology and production capability from the sales reduces the

Canada-United States Defence Production Sharing Procurement 1959-1971

—Millions of Dollars—

	1959	1960	1961	1962	1963	1964	1965	1966	1967	1968	1969	1970	1971	TOTAL
United States Procurement in Canada														
1. Prime Contracts	51.0	61.0	73.5	177.8	84.7	92.0	149.7	132.4	191.2	223.0	214.3	105.5	107.5	1,663.6
2. Subcontracts	45.3	51.7	69.1	76.5	57.3	74.8	109.8	184.7	116.5	97.0	85.5	121.0	108.8	1,198.0
TOTAL	96.3	112.7	142.6	254.3	142.0	166.8	259.5	317.1	307.7	320.0	299.8	226.5	216.3	2,861.6
Canadian Procurement in the United States														
1. Prime Contracts	47.0	83.3	21.2	30.3	36.8	82.7	36.2	109.2	105.4	11.4cr	38.7	92.1	32.0	703.5
2. Subcontracts	61.2	113.0	73.1	97.1	115.2	90.6	93.9	223.4	188.5	145.6	132.8	130.8	148.6	1,613.8
TOTAL	108.2	196.3	94.3	127.4	152.0	173.3	130.1	332.6	293.9	134.2	171.5	222.9	180.6	2,317.3
Cross Border Balance														
In favour of U.S.	11.9	83.6	48.3	126.9	10.0	6.5	129.4		13.8	185.8	128.3		35.7	544.3
Canada								15.5				3.6		

need to import. Consequently, during the 1960s the Canadian government built up a comfortable trade surplus in defence commodities. Canada was still buying a great deal of defence equipment and supplies abroad, particularly in the United States, but the federal government's persistent efforts to develop a prosperous and competetive defence industry were obviously paying off. The tables show the differences between Canadian procurements abroad and foreign procurements at home.

Canada—Overseas Defence Trade (1962-1967)

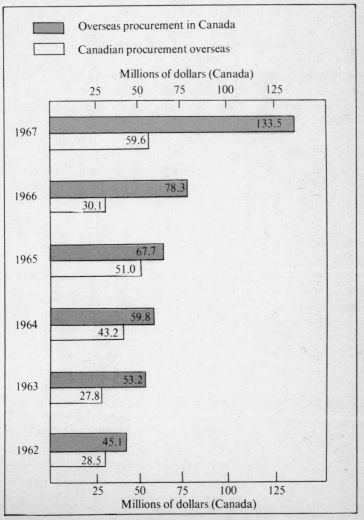

The more than $500 million surplus that had been built up with the United States had become something of an embarrassment to Canadian officials conducting various trade negotiations with that country. The Americans were beginning to suggest that "balance" should be restored and in December 1971, Treasury Board President Charles Drury said that in 1963 he and American Defence Secretary Robert McNamara had reached an "oral understanding" that there should be a "rough balance" in military trade between the two countries,[10] obviously putting Canada under considerable pressure to make some major purchases of defence equipment in the United States.

There were, of course, those in Canada who did not see it quite that way. And while earlier justification of Defence Production Sharing had always concentrated on the economic argument, it now became useful to emphasize the military rationale for the Program. The arrangements, it was argued, were originally made for defence reasons and concerned joint defence programs such as NORAD and NATO. References were made to the statement in the House of Commons on May 1, 1959, by Raymond O'Hurley, the then Minister of Defence Production: "The key provision of this new approach is that Canadian supplies which relate to specific programs of mutual interest to the two governments will be free from all the limitations which we are normally imposed under the Buy America Act."[11]

The argument continued that Canada's surplus had been built up in supplying arms for use in Vietnam and did not therefore fall under "specific programs of mutual interest" and should not therefore have to be balanced by equivalent Canadian procurements in the United States. This argument, of course, implied that a balance was in fact required under the main trade of the Defence Sharing Program, even though no such stipulation was included in the original arrangements.

It is perhaps worth noting here that Defence Production Sharing consists only of informal "arrangements;" there is no "agreement" signed between the two governments—a fact that may become relevant if that "rough balance" becomes an issue of contention.

One of the facts of economic life is, of course, that the more successful a particular enterprise becomes, the more dependent particular individuals, regions, and the economy in general become on its continued operation and growth. The defence industry is no exception.

The Eleventh Annual Report of the Standing Committee on Defence states that the export sale of defence equipment to the United States, at its current rate, means that over 150 Canadian companies are dependent in whole or in part on these sales. Employment for an estimated 13,000 to 15,000 people is wholly attributable to the major contracts originating from this program. In addition, an estimated 110,000 people are engaged in varying degree, in employment associated with these contracts.[12]

Professor Rosenbluth concludes that "although the over-all proportion of defence output and employment to total output and employment is very low, there are particular firms, industries, regions and occupational groups that are highly dependent on defence."[13] His subject is the economic consequences of disarmament so that his calculations include all defence expenditures for equipment by the Canadian Armed Forces and foreign sales.

Defence contracts, he points out, are concentrated in a small number of firms, some of which are highly dependent upon defence contracts (e.g., Canadian Aviation Electronics and members of the Hawker-Siddeley group); for others, such as Imperial Oil and the CPR, even though they participate in defence work, it constitutes only a small part of their business.

In some cases, entire industries are heavily dependent upon defence expenditures. In 1960, 89 per cent of the Canadian aircraft industry's sales were the result of defence expenditures. The figures for the electronics industry were 41 per cent; ammunition and explosives, 25 per cent; ships, 21 per cent; instruments, 19 per cent; and tanks-automotive, 1 per cent. For all of these industries, with the exception of automotive, major cuts in defence expenditures without any planning to switch to other kinds of production would jeopardize their survival.

As far as regional dependence on defence expenditures is concerned, says Rosenbluth, the Maritime provinces and the Yukon and Northwest Territories have a much higher concentration of defence contracts and defence employment (including the armed forces) than other areas. Significant political pressure exists to maintain this expenditure, particularly in the Maritimes, because of their chronic unemployment and poverty.

High local concentration of defence expenditures, Professor

Roseenbluth's study shows, are found in the vicinity of armed force bases in New Brunswick, Nova Scotia, Alberta, Ontario, Quebec, Prince Edward Island, and Manitoba, as well as in the cities of Halifax, Victoria, Ottawa, and Montreal. Except for Montreal, however, the local concentrations are mainly due to concentrations of armed forces personnel, although in Halifax, Ottawa, and Victoria, defence contracts play an important secondary part. The major part of the contract expenditure is concentrated in the larger cities where it constitutes a very small proportion of total business.

The Customers

The promotion of a prosperous Canadian defence industry is undertaken almost entirely from economic motives; a defence industry, besides directly creating jobs and improving the country's trade balance, is presumed to create technical sophistication and to leave in its wake a trail of improved and increased non-military exports. But the sales of fighter aircraft or electronic guidance systems for even the smallest of rockets are not only economic transactions—they also represent political decisions. The sale of the tools of war must finally be reconciled with foreign policy, no small accomplishment when that foreign policy makes pious rhetoric about opposing violent solutions to political problems a central theme, even though there remains little evidence of any over-all design.

Canada, of course, has tried to reconcile its reputation as a peace keeper with the export of the weapons of war by invoking the singularly unimaginative claim that we sell only weapons of defence. They are to be sold only to friends and when nations are in a state of belligerence, neither side gets Canadian guns—although one would have thought that to be the time the question of defence would be most pertinent.

The export of most Canadian-produced military commodities is regulated by export permits issued by the Department of Industry, Trade and Commerce in conjunction with the Department of External Affairs. The permits, according to the 1954 Export and Import Permits Act, are:

To ensure that arms and ammunition, implements or munitions of war, naval, army or air stores, or any articles deemed capable of being converted thereinto or made useful in the production thereof or otherwise having a strategic nature or value will not be made available to any destination wherein their use might be detrimental to Canada.

In addition, the permits are "to ensure that there is an adequate supply and distribution of such articles in Canada for defence or other needs." Not all equipment sold to defence agencies is included in the Export Control list established by the Act, and certain items on the list do not require permits if sold to Britain or the United States. Permission for the sale of technical knowledge (production licences, in other words), for example, is required only if the item in question was developed with government finances.

Canada has a publicly stated policy, but not a legal requirement, that no arms should be supplied to countries in conflict. But that, obviously, is a policy that is rather selectively applied. Canadian arms were sold to the United States for use in Vietnam, to Malaysia during the confrontation with Indonesia, to India following the war with China, and to both Greece and Turkey. Embargoes have been placed by Canada on Israel and the Arab states, on India and Pakistan after 1965, on Nigeria during the Civil War, on South Africa and Rhodesia. Canada also insisted that it would not supply arms to Portugal which could be used in Africa—at best, a claim of dubious worth.

But the embargoes themselves are selective. Until 1967, Canada refused to supply "significant military equipment" to Israel, the UAR, Lebanon, Jordan, Syria, Iraq, and Saudi Arabia. "Significant military equipment" expressly excluded Caribou aircraft and spares and replacement parts for equipment of which Canada is the sole supplier, notably Pratt and Whitney propeller engines. After 1967, the embargo was extended to cover Kuwait, Muscat and Oman, Algeria, Tunisia, and Morocco, with the same exemptions. Similarly, despite the embargo on India and Pakistan, Canada continued to provide transport aircraft to India. By the same token, Canada's embargo on South Africa excluded spare parts and non-military vehicles until 1970 (although in 1963 export permission was refused for a large order of trucks because South Africa requested special fittings for gun sightings).

The problem with the claim that only weapons of "defence," and not "aggression," are sold, is, to resort to understatement, that it is naive. One characteristic of military equipment is that it is never retired. What is obsolete for one is an upgrading in military technology for another. No matter how scrupulous Canada may be about who buys our weapons, and that itself is at best debatable, there is no guarantee against them ending up in some war—inevitably making the matter of defence or aggression a moot issue.

A case in point is the 1965 India-Pakistan War. An official of the International Defence Programs Branch explained, with some dismay, that "it's hard to sell offensive equipment to developing countries" (because of the External Affairs Department's refusal to grant export permits for such sales), but in this case it happened.

Despite the international arms embargo imposed upon Pakistan and India following the outbreak of fighting over Kashmir in 1965, a fleet of Canadian-made Sabre jets turned up in Pakistan. The incident dates back to 1957 when West Germany bought 225 F-86 Sabre jets from Canada. By 1965, the Luftwaffe had moved up to the F-104G Starfighter and was shopping about for a buyer for its phased-out Sabres. With the fleet of Sabres in mind, an arms-buying delegation from Iran arrived in Bonn shortly after the September 22 Indo-Pakistani ceasefire.[14]

The delegation, which included an armaments expert of the Pakistani forces, expressed an interest in buying 90 F-86s; and the Germans agreed to sell under certain conditions. The conditions in this case were governed by the United States resale control procedure, requiring that West Germany (the current seller) obtain permission from Canada (the manufacturer and original seller) who, in turn, was to obtain permission from the United States (in this case the licenser and government in control). The American State Department insists that in the case of the controversial Sabres, it received assurances from both Canada and West Germany that the aircraft were intended for use by the Iranian air force, and so the deal was approved.

But soon the jets began to appear in Pakistan. "A diplomatic scramble began," writes George Thayer. "Washington queried Ottawa who queried Bonn who queried Teheran. A crisis was averted when the planes were returned to Iran—although as late as March 1967, it could not be stated categorically that all of them had in fact been returned."[15]

It was a clear case, says Thomas Land,[16] of evasion, with Canadian assistance, of the international arms embargo which Canada had supported at the United Nations. And one of the reasons it could happen, Land argues, was Ottawa's acquiescence in leaving the task of inspecting the use of Canadian-manufactured weapons to American military officers. Top United States Defense Department officials, he says, have since acknowledged that no American military "end-use" inspection had taken place in either India or Pakistan during the crucial two-year period. In other words, no one bothered to check whether the Canadian-made aircraft were being used for the purpose for which they had been provided—even after the planes turned up in Pakistan, ostensibly for "repair."

Despite the case of the Canadian Sabres, Canada does have a policy of requiring end-use agreements, but the extent to which these can actually be enforced is questionable. These conditions were described as follows by J. A. Jerome, Parliamentary Secretary to the President of the Privy Council, in reply to a question in the House of Commons in 1971:

> Terms of sale to foreign governments regarding future use of Canadian defence commodities are governed by the following conditions:-
>
> a) Commodities manufactured under license or developed as co-operative research, development and production projects, require the consent of co-developers both as to the sale and restrictions on disposal to third countries (in other words, permission from the U.S. must be obtained in these instances).
>
> b) Where an export permit is required under the Export and Import Permits Acts, the applicant in his application is required to state the country in which the goods are to be consumed or finally remain, after satisfying himself as far as reasonably possible that the goods will enter into the economy of such country and will not be trans-shipped or diverted therefrom.[17]

And in reply to the supplementary question, "Are guarantees required on the resale to other countries of weapons systems involving Canadian-made components and, if so, what are they?", Mr. Jerome said: "Except as indicated above, no restrictions are placed on the resale to other countries of weapons systems containing Canadian-made components."

The policy requiring end-use agreements is neither precisely defined nor rigidly enforced. Although such a policy would appear to be essential if the claim to sell only "defensive" weapons were to have any credibility, Canada neglected to exercise its right of reclaim to prevent West Germany's resale of the Sabre fighters referred to above, and end-use agreements are not required for all

types of military equipment. The re-export of combat aircraft produced in Canada require Canadian permission, but no such requirement exists for transport aircraft or some types of support
equipment. If the equipment is produced under licence from a
foreign country, then Canada must herself acquire permission to
export.

The fact is, of course, that no guarantees are possible concerning
the full life of a piece of military equipment. Canadians have no
effective control over the ultimate destination, and certainly no
control over the use, of the weapons they export. The example of
the Canadian F-86 Sabre jets puts the lie to the claim that defence
exports can be justified with the American Defense Department as-
sertion that arms sales are designed to "promote the defensive
strength of our allies, consistent with our political-economic objectives." The exporting country simply cannot control that.

The two branches of Canadian officialdom most directly involved with arms exports, trade and external affairs, use differing
and essentially conflicting arguments to justify their endeavours.
Trade officials argue that arms producers meet an accepted international demand and cannot themselves be made responsible for the
ultimate use or destination of their products. No manufacturer or
vendor, they say, can determine where and how his product will be
used.

The president of Computing Devices, Bruce Daubney, relied on
the same basic argument when he told a reporter:

> We wouldn't be around here very long if we held very strong
> views about what we produce and what its used for. Every-
> body would like to think that their products go into defence
> production but sometimes that doesn't happen. You know
> equipment is built specifically for an aircraft but you don't
> know where the aircraft is used.
>
>   ... If we don't provide the equipment someone else is
> going to, so it might as well be a Canadian company.[18]

And in a reference to the attitude of trade officials, Joseph Long of
Canadian Arsenals said: "If we're sending any kind of munitions
to the United States—shells or anything else—the general response the government gives is that its not up to us what they (the
purchasers) do with the equipment."[19]

But the external affairs officials argue precisely the opposite.
Their position in support of defence exports is based almost en-

tirely on the claim that the vendor can in fact determine how and where his product will be used. External affairs spokesmen say that Canada sells only weapons of defence, with the implication that the vendor has a responsibility to see that his products are used only for defensive purposes. Arms exports to the United States even throughout the peak years of the Vietnam war, were defended on the grounds that they were part of the requirements of continental defence and of the North Atlantic defence alliance.

The fact is that both arguments have been proven wrong. The manufacturers' claim that they don't know where their products will finally be used is discredited by the revelations by groups such as Montreal's Project Anti-War that Canadian firms have collaborated with the United States Defence Contract Administrative Service office in Ottawa to route shipments to Vietnam, for example. Project Anti-War obtained documents showing that Wire Rope Industries had shipped steel chains and wire ropes to various bases in Vietnam via Plattsburg, New York, and Delaware, even though it held no export permit for Vietnam.[20]

Indeed, the Department of Industry, Trade and Commerce made a special point in this case of collaborating to circumvent External Affairs requirements for export permits. On February 27, 1973, an official of the Department of Industry, Trade and Commerce wrote to Wire Rope Industries:

> I am writing further to our recent discussions concerning difficulties that can arise when a Canadian company is asked to bid on a U.S. defence requirement that is to be delivered to south-east Asia. The difficulties occur because Canadian law requires that an export permit be granted for shipment of defence material to such countries, and in some instances the permit will not be issued.
>
> For several years this problem has been recognized and the U.S. Defence Department has instructed its procurement officers that Canadian firms must not be asked to make such shipments. Alternative shipping instructions are available from the U.S. Defence Contract Administration Services Office (DCASO) in Ottawa.
>
> Should your company be asked to respond to such a solicitation, please advise this office and we will endeavor to have the consignment point changed.

And the external affairs claim, that only arms exports for defensive purposes are allowed, is discredited on two counts. In the first place, as already argued, military equipment is rarely retired. Instead it is passed on down the line from country to country as each upgrades its military technology. The manufacturer cannot determine how the customer who does not actually use the product in warfare, will eventually dispose of it. The chances are it will be sold to another country and so on down the line until it is impossible to say in whose arsenal it will finally end up. Besides that one nation's defence is another's aggression, and to say that one can build an airplane only for defensive purposes is patently absurd.

But the argument is also discredited by the fact that in the instances where some control over the destination of the product could be exercised, the Canadian government has not appeared particularly careful or keen to do so. The case of the F-86 Sabre jets to Pakistan is one example. Another is the case of Wire Rope Industries just referred to, and another is the possibility of the sale of a small arms munitions plant to Thailand. In 1973, Thai army representatives visited a Canadian Industries Ltd. explosives plant in Valleyfield, the Metal Industries Ltd. plant in Noranda which had a brass rolling mill for sale, and Valcartier Industries Ltd, near Quebec City, which specializes in small arms and ammunition.[21] The visit of the Thais to Canada was a hush-hush affair, and for good reason. Thailand's military dictatorship could be assumed to employ such munitions in the suppression of legitimate dissent— although they might prefer to call it subversion—and Canadian external affairs officials would be hard-pressed to place the sale in the category of legitimate weapons of defence.

But few events demonstrate so effectively the naïveté of the Canadian claim that it sells only weapons of defence as does India's detonation of an atomic device. Canada essentially trained India's nuclear scientists and provided the atomic reactor, albeit through an agreement prohibiting the development of a bomb. Through it all, Canada apparently assumed that India's assurances that it had only peaceful purposes in mind could be accepted at face value. Exclaimed a somewhat wide-eyed Mitchell Sharp, "What concerns us about this matter is that the Indians, not withstanding their great economic difficulties, should have devoted tens or hundreds of millions of dollars to the creation of a nuclear device for a nuclear explosion."

The external affairs minister should not have been so amazed. India has never signed the Nuclear Non-Proliferation Treaty, and one wonders why Canada did not question the credibility of Indian claims in the light of her refusal to ratify the treaty.

Whether in spite of her good intentions or because of the lack of them, Canadian arms exports do not all serve defensive purposes and can in fact be assumed to contribute substantially to the threat of war and military devastation—Canada's contribution to the expansion of the "nuclear club" being one example.

In 1970, countries which purchased defence commodities from Canada were:[22]

a) Insofar as the Canadian Commercial Corporation is concerned:

Australia	France	Pakistan
Belgium	India	Portugal
Botswana	Kenya	Singapore
Brazil	Malaysia	Sweden
Britain	Netherlands	United States
Burma	New Zealand	West Germany
Brunei	Norway	Zambia
Denmark		

b) Insofar as the Department of Industry, Trade and Commerce is concerned (In addition to the countries indicated above, the following countries made direct purchases from Canadian companies during the calendar year 1970):

Argentina	Jamaica
Chile	Japan
Columbia	Muscat & Oman
Ecuador	Panama
Finland	Peru
Ghana	South Africa (Terminated Nov. 2/70)
Greece	Spain
Italy	

A prominent customer of the Canadian defence industry that is omitted from the above list is, of course, Canada. While Canadian armed forces have in the last decade spent in excess of $200 million annually, on the average, for military equipment (and planned in the next decade to spend more than $365 million annually), Canada is by most standards a very modest consumer of weapons of war. Measuring total military spending in relation to Gross National Product, Canada is at the very bottom of a list of the thirteen North Atlantic Treaty Organization countries which maintain military forces (Iceland does not have any, and Luxembourg can hardly be counted since its one infantry battalion operates with the Belgium army). Currently Canada spends about 2 per cent of her GNP on defence, compared to the NATO average of 3.6 per cent.[23]

John Gellner says that a widely accepted rule of thumb for capital expenditure for military forces is that they should make up about 30 per cent of all defence costs. In Canada, the proportion has regularly been below 15 per cent and even after a major increase in capital expenditures originally planned for 1974, it would have reached only 19 per cent of the military budget.[24] (Procurement fell from 57 per cent of the defence budget during the Korean War to only 13 per cent in 1964—an important factor in the increased efforts to boost exports.)

Whether or not one agrees with Mr. Gellner that this is a deplorable state of affairs—that the Canadian Armed Forces badly need a set of new war machines—there is no denying that Canada is not in possession of a military establishment of unusual proportions. In fact, many feel that a great deal more should be spent by Canada. An opposition defence critic warns darkly of increases in Communist forces and urges the government to double its manpower commitments to NATO and to stock up on new equipment accordingly.

There is not much danger of the government sending more troops to NATO, but there is no doubt that a major "upgrading" of the equipment of the Canadian forces is among the ambitions of the Defence Department.

Defence planners are busily planning capital expenditures in excess of $2 billion, and while they may be devoting a great deal of attention to the relative military merits of various equipment, the minister of defence has left little doubt that he sees the exercise primarily in economic terms. A headline in *The Financial Post* of July 22, 1972, is indicative of the rationale behind major equipment purchases by the Canadian Armed Forces: "$600 Million Lever to Reshape Industry."

The headline referred to a proposed order of long-range patrol aircraft to replace 33 Argus aircraft now in service with Maritime command.* Although budget restrictions are likely to result in some trimming of the order, the government either wants the major

* When reports first began appearing about this aircraft order, the price referred to was $500 million (*The Financial Post*, January 8, 1972). By that summer, the price had escalated to $600 million (*The Financial Post*, July 22, 1972), and in 1974 the estimated price for the same order was $1 billion

work on any new planes to be done by the Canadian aircraft and electronics industry (the latter producing the surveillance equipment with which these planes will be outfitted), or would buy the planes elsewhere, in Britain or the United States, on the condition that "offset" orders are received—that is, that similar orders be placed by the supplying country in Canada.

And in September 1974 the Department of Defence let it be known that it was shopping around for about 150 multi-purpose aircraft at a cost that could exceed $1 billion.

The new fleet was being proposed to replace three different types of combat plane currently in use: the CF-101 Voodoo interceptor, used for home defence; the CF-5 ground support plane also based in Canada; and the CF-104 fighter-bomber, based with Canadian forces in Europe. "Nobody can afford to specialize any longer to the extent of having separate planes for three different roles," said Lt. Gen. William Carr, Deputy Chief of Defence staff. "Nor is it any longer necessary, because technological breakthroughs have given planes a multi-purpose capability."

Canadian industry would, of course, be given another boost through such an order. Since several European countries were looking for a similar plane, hopes were expressed for a joint procurement program. If a standard plane could be decided upon, the airframes might be produced in each country individually, with the production of components, including electronic equipment, being divided.[25]

The Minister of Defence, James Richardson, who used his earlier cabinet post of Minister of Supply and Services for an aggressive campaign to decentralize federal government purchasing to give western provinces a larger piece of the action, has brought the same crusade to the defence portfolio. As far as he is concerned, the $2 billion airplane orders must not only result in substantial Canadian production but substantial business for the west.

Mr. Richardson devoted the major part of his first speech in the House of Commons after the 1972 election to the need for "Canadian content" in equipment purchases by his department. The strategic value of the equipment received no mention, but the potential economic benefits for western Canada were very much on his mind.[26] It is notable also that questions in the House of Commons about the order for the Argus replacement concentrated almost exclusively on on the production arrangements rather than on their strategic importance.

James Earys has argued, in fact, that the anti-submarine role which the Argus replacement would be expected to fill, is, in the idiom of military strategists, "destabilizing." Referring to the four new destroyer ships which the Canadian forces are in the process of acquiring, Earys says that an anti-submarine warfare system upsets the nuclear balance. He argues that because the Soviet submarine force represents a virtually invulnerable "second strike capability," it contributes to the stability by eliminating any incentive for a pre-emptive first strike.* Consequently, the development of a defence against the submarines is destabilizing because it undermines second-strike capability.

> Therefore our Maritime Command, so far from developing and perfecting ASW (anti-submarine warfare) techniques, ought to switch to ice-breaking. The best defence is no defence. To perfect the defence is to degrade the deterrent. To degrade the deterrent is to destabilize the system. The thing to do with the Soviet missile submarine is, in the expressive phrase of the Cape Breton fisherman, "Leave 'er lay where Jesus flang 'er."[27]

Militarily, therefore, the value of the new planes is not certain. Even General Dudley Allen, who headed a task force to evaluate four industry proposals for the aircraft, has expressed doubt about the primary role of the aircraft. It is unlikely, he is reported to have said, that Soviet submarine missiles are pointed at Canada and it is unlikely that Canada could knock out the Soviet submarines if they were.[28]

What is not in doubt, however, is their economic significance and Defence Minister Richardson's determination to spread some of those benefits among his constituents in Manitoba and points west.

The Products and the Producers

The products provided by Canada's defence industry run the full range, from men's underwear to bombs; the *Canadian Defence*

---

* In the lexicon of nuclear strategists, a second strike capability refers to the ability to launch a successful retaliatory attack, the measure of success being the ability to inflict damage after suffering an initial attack from the enemy. A pre-emptive first strike, on the other hand, is an initial attack designed to destroy the enemy before he gets a chance to even reach for his nuclear holster. It is not a good idea to launch a pre-emptive first strike against an enemy that has a second-strike capability.

Products catalogue even tells the prospective buyer that "combat underwear is dyed olive green to reduce camouflage problems when the items are drying in the field."[29] Underwear, however, is not the mainstay of the industry and officials of the International Defence Programs Branch provide 1966 figures as the most recent available for the precise details of Canadian exports. Of sales of $317.1 million to the United States that year, 50 per cent were aircraft components, 32.7 per cent navigation and communication equipment, 10 per cent components for ammunition, 2.6 per cent vehicles and components, and 3 per cent miscellaneous, including research in Canadian universities. Each category, of course, includes a large number of individual items and companies which make them.

Aircraft are, as the above figures indicate, a major item (total production of the aerospace industry in 1968 was $800 million, of which $500 million was exported—with a ratio of civil to military production of roughly 1:1[30]) and various types are displayed in the catalogue. Canadair Limited of Montreal and de Havilland Aircraft of Canada Limited are the most prominent in the field. Canadair builds the CF-5 Tactical Support Fighter which is said to combine the qualities of a fighter plane with those of a reconnaissance aircraft by an alternative camera equipped nose section which can be exchanged, in a rapid change process, for the regular nose. It is now in use by the Royal Netherlands Air Force as well as the Canadian Armed Forces. The company has also developed a Tilt-Wing Aircraft (CL-84) that can be flown as a helicopter or conventional aircraft. The plane is not yet in full production, but evaluation models for the Canadian Armed Forces are being built. Its military applications are expected to comprise combat support, personnel, and cargo transport, reconnaissance, search and rescue, helicopter escort, and communications, from both land bases and aircraft carriers. Canadair's series of combat aircraft produced under American licence include, in addition to the CF-5 and the CL-84, the Sabre 6, T-33 Trainer, CF-100, CF-105, CF-104.

De Havilland specializes in short take-off and landing (STOL) aircraft and its DHC-4 Caribou, a transport vehicle, is now in its fourteenth year of production. Over 300 Caribou are now flying with the following services: United States Air Force, Canadian Armed Forces, Royal Australian Air Force, Ghana Air Force, Zambia Air Force, Kenya Air Force, Kuwait Air Force, Tanzania Air Force, Abu Dhabi Defence Force, Muscat and Oman, Guyana Airways, Federal Republic of the Cameroons, Uganda

Police, Malaysia Air Force, Indian Air Force, Thailand Border Patrol Police, Spanish Air Force, United Nations Emergency Force, as well as by a few private users. De Havilland has produced a series of well-known Canadian-designed trainers and transports.

One company that appears to come as close as any to making good on the claim that their military sales are for defensive purposes only is Leigh Instruments Ltd. Calling itself "the world's leading supplier of downed aircraft position indicators," the company credits this one product with 40 per cent of its sales. A company spokesman admitted that their product was probably used in Vietnam by the Americans, but argued that this was an acceptable use because the aircraft outfitted with the position indicators were carrying troops. The company, he says, does not manufacture war material: "The company has a moral obligation. To the best of my knowledge of the company's background every product has fallen into the area of safety for flight."[31] Others have less of a claim to moral responsibility.

Computing Devices also sells to the American military and among its products are navigation systems for the United States Navy's A7 D-E, a carrier-based fighter bomber that was used in Vietnam. The system is also used in F-4s and F-111s, aircraft which were employed in Vietnam. The company received more than $11 million worth of contracts from the American Defence Department between 1970 and 1972. In the Canadian catalogue of war materials, it also advertises a list of products including gun direction computers, guided missile components and launchers, several kinds of communication, detection, and coherent radiation equipment, as well as photo reconnaissance systems.[32]

A substantial portion of Litton Industries' sales of about $11 million in unclassified defence contracts with the American Defence Department between 1969 and 1972 comprised weapons release computer sets for F-4 Phantom fighters used extensively in Vietnam. The company's initial navigation systems, for F-111s as well as F-4s, are said to "combine accuracy and versatility with the ruggedness required for equipment operating in a combat environment." About 2000 of these systems were produced in Canada during the 1960s.[33]

A full range of clothing for protection against chemical and biological warfare is also available from Canadian suppliers. Included in this is a special Canadian-designed mask to provide protection "from all known NBCW (Nuclear Biological and Chemical Warfare) toxicological agents to the respiratory tract, the face and eyes of combat and support personnel of the Armed Forces."[34] The mask and clothing are one of the results of the CBW research carried on by the Defence Research Board.

Obviously there is a great deal more. Electronic and communications equipment are prominent as well. The task of identifying the companies that build these products is by no means a modest one. Montreal's "Project Anti-War," under the direction of Professor S. J. Noumoff of McGill's Department of Political Science, has made a major effort and in October 1972, published "A preliminary report concerning Canadian economic involvement with the Pentagon and the war in Indochina" entitled *How to Make a Killing*. The report is an attempt to identify those Canadian companies active in defence production, and particularly those carrying out contracts for the United States Defence Department.

The report identifies 654 defence manufacturers in Canada but efforts to trace their ownership was successful for only 377. Of these, 173 (54.6 per cent) are American-owned, 109 (34.4 per cent), Canadian-owned. The study group then went further to identify those companies which had received contracts from the United States Defence Department between 1967 and 1972 inclusive. These numbered 237 and would have to be considered among the more active in the defence industry. A copy of the list in the report is included as Appendix II.

Officials in the International Defence Programs Branch say they consider there to be about 500 companies operating in Canada as defence manufacturers. Of these, only about 150 actually produce goods for sale to defence departments in any given year and the majority of sales are concentrated in about 30-40 companies.

One of the companies in the latter group may be of more than passing interest. Canadian taxpayers got directly into the business of military communications in July 1972, when the federal government purchased controlling interest in Radio Engineering Products Limited of Montreal and Campbellton, New Brunswick. At the time of the takeover, the company was simply referred to as a manufacturer of "sophisticated communications equipment for the international market," which, translated, means the company manufactures telephone carrier equipment for use in the "field" by the United States military. An official of the Department of Industry, Trade and Commerce said at the time that there are other customers, including the Swedish military, but admitted that the company could not possibly survive without the American military market.

The Canadian government got involved when the company, founded in 1946 by two Canadian brothers, ran into a spate of bad luck. Things, however, were not always that tough. Charles and Sidney Fisher put $30,000 into the venture back in 1946 and in 1969 sold it to the New York firm of Nytronics for a reported $65 million.[35]

An unusual series of developments in the electronics industry a number of years ago brought Radio Engineering Products into prominence. The "telephone carrier equipment" referred to above is actually a device which is in effect placed between conventional telephone equipment and radio equipment and enables a number of telephone circuits to be fed into a single radio circuit. There are basically two methods by which this is achieved: one is called a time division method and the other a frequency division method. It seems that the conventional wisdom, particularly in the United States military, was that the time division method represented the wave of the future, at least as far as "sophisticated communications equipment" was concerned. The Fisher brothers of Canada, however, predicted that the time division method would be fraught with problems and while everyone else was following the conventional wisdom, Radio Engineering Products stuck with the frequency division method.

As a trade official recounted the story, the wave of the future turned out to be with the latter, and when the United States military finally switched, Radio Engineering Products of Canada was virtually the only manufacturer that could meet the demand.

Unfortunately, as the department official went on to explain, electronics is a high risk field and since the takeover by Nytronics of New York in 1969, neither company had done particularly well. In fact, massive losses were incurred and the Canadian subsidiary was unable to pay its tax bill to the Canadian government—not for want of effort by the federal government, it might be added, which has poured several millions of dollars worth of "incentive grants" into the company since the mid-1960s. The government takeover was said to be temporary and designed to protect the 150 jobs that were at stake at the time. At the time of the takeover, the government said the company would continue to manufacture its "sophisticated communications equipment" for the "international market."

The cost of acquisition of about 99 per cent of the shares was not disclosed, but the *Globe and Mail* reported that the company had been in arrears of about $3,900,000 in federal taxes.[36] Add to that the amounts provided in incentive grants and one gains some appreciation of just how badly the Department of Industry, Trade and Commerce wishes to maintain a competetive defence industry in the country. In mid-1974, the federal government was still looking for a buyer. The Canadian Development Corporation denied that it had any interest in acquiring REP. The most likely buyer for the firm is I.T.T., since the company's best hopes for future sales currently lie in a newly-developed unit of multiplexer equipment for use by I.T.T.'s Defence Communications Division.

The government has traditionally justified its arms export industry on grounds that if Canada is to supply her own needs in the most economical terms, she must be capable of selling enough of its products on the international market to enable efficient production for domestic needs. In this case, however, there are no domestic requirements—all production is for export.

The case is revealing also in that it demonstrates the extent to which Canadian industry is dependent upon circumstances originating outside Canadian control. Radio Engineering Products, now with the Canadian government as the primary shareholder, is exclusively dependent on American military planners.

Since the acquisition of REP, the federal government has taken steps to acquire two more firms in the war business. In May 1974, the government announced it would exercise its option to purchase de Havilland Aircraft of Canada Limited, at an estimated cost of $38 million, and would seek an option to purchase Canadair Limited at a cost of $32 million. The moves were said to be motivated by intentions to reshape and repatriate the Canadian aviation industry and the government immediately offered the two firms for sale to Canadian private interests. In announcing the prospective takeovers, the Minister of Industry, Trade and Commerce said that in the past the growth and development of the two companies were impaired by the fact that they were foreign-owned and controlled, and that they had no independent authority to make decisions or to enter into inter-company arrangements for meaningful rationalization. In some aspects, he said, they were often in competition with their parent companies.

The object was to protect Canadian jobs and enhance the industry's competetive position. The fact that the industry is the war industry did not appear to be a factor in the decision. The minister said he wanted to assure employees at both plants that the action by the government would provide a basis, under Canadian owner-ship and control, for achieving greater production stability and security of employment by ensuring an internationally competetive manufacturing capability in the Canadian aerospace industry.[37]

Notes

[1] "Defence Industry Productivity Program," Pamphlet by the Depart-ment of Industry, Trade and Commerce, (Ottawa: Queen's Printer), p. 4.

[2] *Defence Export Shippers' Guide* (United States—Canada Defence Production Sharing Program), Department of Industry, Trade and Commerce (Ottawa: Queen's Printer), p. 5.

[3] "Canada's Honest Broker," *Canadian Business*, November 1969.

[4] *Ottawa Citizen*, August 26, 1974.

[5] *House of Commons Debates*, November 26, 1973.

[6] "Quick Reference on Incentive and Development Programs for Ca-nadian Industry," a pamphlet by Department of Industry, Trade and Commerce (Ottawa: Queen's Printer), p. 8.

[7] *How to Make a Killing:* A preliminary report concerning Canadian Economic Involvement with the Pentagon and the War in Indo-China (Montreal: Project Anti-War, October 1972), p. 128.

[8] *House of Commons Debates*, February 26, 1969.

[9] From tables prepared by the International Defence Programs Branch, "Value of United States and Overseas Procurement in Can-ada and Canadian Procurement in United States and Overseas."

[10] *House of Commons Debates*, December 1971.

[11] *House of Commons Debates*, May 1, 1959.

[12] "Eleventh Report," *op. cit.*

[13] The following brief account is based substantially on Rosenbluth, *op. cit.*, the chapter entitled "Groups and Areas Dependent on Defence Expenditures."

[14] George Thayer, *The War Business* (New York: Scanion and Schus-ter, 1969), p. 203.

[15] Ibid., p. 204.

[16] Thomas Land, "Canada 'Making a Killing' in Arms Trade," *Mon-treal Star*, July 12, 1969.

[17] *House of Commons Debates*, September 8, 1971.

[18] *Ottawa Citizen*, August 24, 1974.

[19] Ibid.

[20] Ibid.

[21] *Last Post*, March 1974.

[22] *House of Commons Debates*, September 8, 1971.

[23] John Gellner, "The Lean Years Haunt the Fattening-up Plan," *Globe and Mail*, October 16, 1973.

[24] Ibid.

[25] *Globe and Mail*, September 10, 1974.

[26] *House of Commons Debates*, January 16, 1973.

[27] *Saturday Night*, May 1970.

[28] *Globe and Mail*, October 22, 1973.

[29] *Canadian Defence Priorities, op. cit.*, p. 334.

[30] *The Arms Trade with the Third World*, SIPRI, p. 293.

[31] *Ottawa Citizen*, August 24, 1974.

[32] Ibid.

[33] Ibid.

[34] "Canadian Personal NBCW Protective Material," Pamphlet by the Department of Industry, Trade and Commerce (Ottawa: Queen's Printer).

[35] *Globe and Mail*, July 15, 1972.

[36] Ibid.

[37] *Globe and Mail*, May 28, 1974.

4 Defence Research

My contention is that it is very difficult to identify what is civilian and what is military research in many instances; that a lot of civilian research leads to military innovation, and a lot of military research leads to civilian innovation.

The Minister of Industry,
Trade and Commerce

In one sense any examination of Canadian industry devoted to military production should really begin with defence research. Technological research is the foundation of any progressive manufacturing industry, and military manufacturing is no exception. Canada would not be in a position to export highly sophisticated defence products had someone not set out deliberately to develop such products. Much of the basic research and development for the Canadian arms export business is, of course, carried out in the United States. The pattern of foreign ownership in Canadian manufacturing generally, applies to the defence industry as well and much of Canadian production is carried out by Canadian subsidiaries of products licensed by the parent American companies. But research has not been ignored in Canada and the federal government provides the industry both with expertise, through institutions such as the Defence Research Board, and direct funds for private research and development. (Some of the major programs for pre-production development assistance were described above.)

Canadian officials charged with justifying this country's scientific research activities devoted to military purposes, usually end up insisting that defence research is really indistinguishable from other industrial research. The question has rarely become the subject for debate in the House of Commons, but the last time it did the then Minister of Industry, Trade and Commerce, Jean-Luc Pepin, put it this way:

> My contention is that it is very difficult to identify what is civilian research and what is military research in many instances; that a lot of civilian research leads to military innovation, and a lot of military research leads to civilian innovation.[1]

The intended implication, of course, is that the label one puts on scientific and technological research is irrelevant since the results are quite unpredictable.

A special United Nations study, however, on the "Economic and Social Consequences of the Arms Race and of Military Expenditures," concluded that the results of scientific research engaged in for special military purposes are not nearly so unpredictable or innocent. In fact, the study concluded that behind the spiralling arms race is not so much the threat of military attack but the work of the defence research scientist:

> The arms race has in fact become essentially a technological race, the achievements of one side spurring the other to improve on the technological advances which it might have made itself. Sometimes the spur comes not from some clearly defined threat but from an imagined technical advance made by the other side. Secrecy in military affairs makes it inevitable that a potential enemy will usually be suspected of being stronger than he actually is. Consequently both sides strive continuously to improve the quantity and quality of their arms. So it is that the arms race becomes based on the "hypothesis of the worst case," that is to say, one of two sides designs its programme of development on the assumption that its rival could, if it so decided, be the stronger.[2]

And the Stockholm International Peace Research Institute adds:

> Trends in the amount of resources devoted to military Research and Development, and in the activities undertaken

with these resources, need to be followed with close attention because they are a major determinant of the nature of future world armaments.[3]

One of the most recent, and horrifying, examples of the techno-logical escalation of the arms race is the rapid development of laser technology—to which Canadian defence research scientists have made important contributions. A 1974 report issued by the Inter-national Red Cross, on "weapons that may cause unnecessary suf-fering or have indiscriminate side effects," cites lasers as being among those "areas of science which hitherto had made little con-tribution to weapons technology (but which) now have a relevance few would have predicted in earlier decades."

Laser range-finding and target-spotting have been found to be an inexpensive method of improving the accuracy of weapons de-livery, especially aerial bombs, says the report. Although they still have a relatively low power output, such lasers are capable of de-stroying the human eye at ranges of up to some thousands of metres.

Anyone looking straight into a laser beam risks total destruction of the eyes. The report holds out the prospect that "perhaps in the next several years," laser devices may be used as thermal weapons. Their original power output, once measured in tens of watts, has in a decade been increased ten-thousandfold.[4]

In 1970, the Canadian Defence Research Board's Defence Re-search Establishment Valcartier (DREV), announced a break-through in achieving "high peak power pulses," and following that the research emphasis was on developing further increases in peak power. According to the Board's *Review '73*, "the peak power has since been increased by an order of magnitude each year. At pre-sent, pulses with a peak power of 10,000 MW and of about one nanosecond duration have been obtained."[5]

Now, with the achievement of these very high peak power pul-ses, the emphasis of the DREV program has shifted to developing military applications, and in 1973 the Board hosted a NATO con-ference on laser applications which brought together technical ex-perts from nine countries. The Board has constructed a prototype transportable laser range finder, with the contractural participation of two Canadian companies holding licences to the TEA (Trans-versely Excited Atmospheric) laser patents.[1]

According to the IRC report, there are three basic types of high energy lasers now being developed. The most advanced are gas-dynamic lasers with the most likely application for ground-based weapons or aboard ships. Electro-discharge lasers have similar potential for military purposes, but the greatest potential for multipurpose military use, says the report, is the chemical laser. Though chemical lasers are still in the early stages of development, they have much military interest because little outside energy is required, which means that they may eventually be small and light. Furthermore, they operate at short wavelengths which reduce atmospheric attenuation and increase thermal damage effects.

The military mind sees great potential for lasers. Among their advantages is that they can burn holes in targets, or their radiation can destroy (apart from the human eye) the optical sensors of attacking weapons. They have essentially a zero time of flight, have no mass requiring compensation for inertia, and can be pointed rapidly from target to target.

The IRC report predicts that possibly in ten years, fighter aircraft may have laser guns, and progress may have been made in laser defence systems against missiles, adding:

> Laser light may give rise to severely damaging effects on the human body, including heat, pressure, possible shock waves (both acoustic and ultrasonic) and protein generation in the blood plasma. Tissue ionisation, chemical transformations, and disturbances of the blood circulation may also occur at the impact site.[7]

In fact, "smart bombs", those which were laser-guided, were used in the American raid over Hanoi on Christmas, 1972.

The potential civilian applications of lasers are also impressive. Industry, agriculture and medicine are all fields in which direct uses are already envisioned, and laser fusion is potentially a means to cheap electrical power. But few areas of beneficial technology carry with them such potential for creating human suffering and physical devastation. Besides the direct physical devastation that would result from their use as thermal weapons, their use in missile defence is likely to have major consequences for the present balance of mutual deterrence and to set off renewed efforts towards the technological upgrading of "weapons delivery systems." It is an escalation of the arms race that has little to do with any political/military threat to national security; to recall the statement from the UN study on the arms race quoted above, "The arms race has in fact become essentially a technological race, the achievements of one side spurring the other to improve on the technological advances which it might have made itself." And Canadian research scientists have played no small part in escalating this technological race.

The full impact of technological competition on the arms race becomes clear only after the full scale and extent of defence research is understood. The Stockholm International Peace Research Institute estimates in its 1969-1970 *Yearbook of World Armaments and Disarmament* that at least a quarter of the world total of scientists and engineers who are engaged in research and development are in fact employed on military work, and military research and development probably absorbs some $25 billion of an estimated world total research and development expenditure of some $60 billion.[8]

Considerable managerial talent and technical skill is also absorbed by the armed forces, and in many cases military personnel go through long and extremely expensive courses of training in special educational establishments. The increasing sophistication of weapons always means that whatever the percentage of a national budget which goes to military expenditures, the corresponding percentage in terms of the use of professional scientific manpower for military purposes will be higher.

It is usual, says SIPRI, to find that in countries with developed military industries, the proportion of the labour force of the engineering industry which is absorbed in the production of military equipment is far greater than the percentage of GNP which goes to military expenditures, and that the percentage of all qualified scientists and engineers employed on military research and development is even higher.

The portion of the labour force in Canadian engineering which is absorbed in the development and production of military equipment is not easily ascertained, but there are some indications that a comparatively high proportion of scientific work is employed on military research and development. Some analysts have estimated that over 50 per cent of all federal funds going into research and development are used for military purposes.[9] (During the last half of the 1960s, amounts spent by the government on scientific research and development increased from $277 million to $514 million per annum.[10])

It is not easily established that one-half or more of these funds were devoted to military purposes or led to military development, but it has already been established that at least one-half of the

Department of Industry, Trade and Commerce grants for industrial development goes towards military production. In its industrial development programs, the distinctions between military and non-military use is kept deliberately vague, and in research there is similar obscurity, leading to a rather fatuous statement by a government minister that it is "very difficult to identify what is civilian and what is military research." In the case of laser research there is no such difficulty.

The Industrial Research Assistance Program and the Industrial Research and Development Incentives Program (IRDIA) are examples of grant programs which provide funds for both defence and civilian projects (although they are part of a program of "general incentives" to industry), but when Ed Broadbent (MP for Oshawa riding in Ontario) asked for details about recipients of grants under the IRDIA program, he was told that "Section 13 of the IRDIA Act prevents the disclosure of this information."[11] The Defence Industrial Research Program funded by the Defence Research Board is more directly and exclusively related to defence research and is referred to in more detail below.

SIPRI lists Canada as the Western world's sixth largest spender in military research and development, averaging $89 million (U.S. dollars) in the years 1967 to 1970.[12] But the figure is, to say the least, conservative. SIPRI appears to have used only the Defence Research Board budget and funds distributed under the Defence Industry Productivity Programe to arrive at the figure for total spent on military research and development. That ignores funds acknowledged by officials of the Department of Industry, Trade and Commerce as supporting military research and development, paid out by the government under such programs as the "general incentives to industry for the expansion of scientific research and development," the Industrial Research and Developments Incentives Act, and others. Furthermore, defence contractors are among recipients of grants from the Department of Regional and Economic Expansion. The SIPRI figure also ignores funds received by Canadian firms from the United States and other NATO customers for research and development, and by Canadian universities from the American Defence Department. In addition to public funds spent on research and development, private industry itself funds a substantial amount of military research and development.

It is not possible here to substantiate the claim that 50 per cent of all government spending on scientific research and development

—$514 million in 1970—serves military purposes, but the implied figure of $250 million may well be closer to the amount actually spent than the $80 million accounted for in the Defence Research Board budget and the Defence Industry Productivity Programe.

One reason why the government is able to maintain such a deliberately vague distinction between defence and civilian research is that the production of defence commodities in Canada is strictly a commercial enterprise, like any other in the industrial sector. Neither specific military threats to Canadian security nor equipment orders from the Canadian defence establishment comprise the real *raison d'être* for defence production in this country. Consequently, when the defence research establishment in Canada is called upon to defend its activities, the most seriously advanced argument is always the economic one.

In the 1969 Standing Committee on Finance, Trade and Economic Affairs, D. B. Mundy, Chairman of an Interdepartmental Committee on Defence Export Development (predecessor of the Defence Industry Productivity Program) announced that the government was already netting $10 for every dollar they put into research and that prospective sales indicated returns would increase to about $24:

> I think these figures should be looked at in the light of the fact that research, development and production is a long cycle extending up to about ten years. If you project the sales which we think are virtually certain to come forward out of these developments, not just the ones claimed by the company and give a real good, hard, realistic look at the sort of sales that you could logically expect to come out of that expenditure, our figures indicate that the cost-benefit ratio will work out as twenty-four to one. In other words, we anticipate that from the projects which we have completed, and in which we have spent government funds, there will be a return of $24 in terms of sales for every dollar which we have spent. Those figures we regard as being pretty satisfactory.[13]

The institution that has been a major force in this scientific/commercial venture is the Defence Research Board:

Generally, the Board is concerned with providing scientific advice to the Minister of National Defence, meeting the research requirements of the Canadian Armed Forces, contributing to the collective defence research efforts of our allies, and supporting research of defence interest in Canadian universities and applied research in those Canadian industries that require a defence science and technology input.[14]

That is the official version, and while lip service is paid to various military and security justifications for defence research, DRB spokesmen, when referring to the accomplishments of the Board, invariably cite cases in which the Board's work has led to a commercially successful product.

World War II was the event that triggered emphasis on "war research," as officials of the Defence Research Board refer to it, in Canada. The National Research Council, created in 1916, had over the years conducted some specifically military research but it was not until World War II that the NRC made a major switch into defence research; indeed, virtually all scientific research in Canada switched to war research during that war. The Department of Defence set up eight research and development establishments during the war years and many universities switched their research laboratories over to the war effort.[15] The actual magnitude of this effort is reported by N. J. Godspeed in his official history of the DRB:

At the outbreak of the war the National Research Council had only one laboratory. It had a total staff of some three hundred employees and an annual budget of $900,000. Before the end of hostilities twenty-one additional laboratories were opened, of which eight were permanent research centres. Temporary laboratories for cold weather research were opened at Lake Louise, Jasper, Edmonton, and Saskatoon. Large laboratories were later equipped in Montreal for the Atomic Energy Project, and a permanent establishment was built at Chalk River, Ontario. A cold weather station was opened in Winnipeg for the testing of jet engines, and nine new buildings and wind tunnels were constructed in the Ottawa area for aeronautical and engineering research. By the end of the war the NRC actually had more buildings than it had had scientists in 1939. The scientific and technical staff expanded to nearly two thousand, and during the war the NRC operated twenty major Associate Research Committees and nearly one hundred sub-committees. The closest co-operation was maintained both with universities and with industry, and apart from the work which was being done in the National Research Council's own laboratories there were times when as many as two hundred and eighty active projects were simultaneously under way at thirty other laboratories across Canada.[16]

Virtually the entire scientific community in Canada had been mobilized, and when the war ended, it was felt necessary, therefore, to devise a means to maintain the expertise that had been developed in the field of war research and to return the NRC and the universities to their traditional roles of non-military research.

Those responsible for defence research argued that continuation in that field was required for two basic reasons:

1) Direct war research was considered necessary to be able to make the best possible equipment choices and to shape the most effective defence policies.

2) Defence research was also needed, they argued, to apply and recognize basic research, which had originated elsewhere, for defence purposes. Original researchers would not likely follow through to the defence application of their research and the defence department wanted to maintain a capability to follow up non-military research.

It was therefore decided to create a civilian research agency within the department of defence "to support and anticipate the research requirements of the minister of defence and the armed forces." As a result, in 1947 the Defence Research Board was established.

From the outset the DRB has had an "international" character. "The concept which emerged," according to the Board's 25th anniversary publication, "was that since it was impossible with the resources available to cover all aspects of defence science, Canada should consider her defence technology not as an end in itself, but as a common contribution to that of her allies."[17] It was a repetition of the principle that eventually led to defence production sharing.

This basic concept had two primary effects. In the first instance, it was instrumental in tying Canadian defence policy into the defence policies and interests of the United States. The "common contribution" was maintained by a continuation of the World War II "Technical Co-operation Program," the various clauses of which are a military secret, entered into with the United States, Britain, and Australia. The British had been particularly anxious to have Canada become a research centre for the combined war effort, citing Canada's physical remoteness from the theatre of war, her close relation with the United States and an already established government research organization in support of the request.[18]

After the war the integrated research structure was retained and Canadian defence research offices were established in London and Washington and, later, in Paris, to facilitate the exchange of defence science knowledge. Close links have also been established with the defence science establishments of Australia and New Zealand.

The second major effect of pooling defence research with other countries was that Canada, because of its relatively smaller contribution, became highly specialized. Canada, it was argued, "should initiate only a limited number of defence research projects chosen with a view to utilizing Canadian resources to the best advantage."[19]

Another major policy decision made in those early years which was to have long-term effects upon the focus of scientific research in Canada, was the decision to integrate military research in Canada with Canadian scientific research in general—the main rationale being the familiar argument that military research has many civilian benefits.

Indeed, it has been claimed that, as a general rule, military research more than pays for itself by its civil use. Radar, which was developed primarily as a defence against the *Luftwaffe*, is now regarded as a necessity for civil air lines and for ships at sea. Nuclear fission, which is so terrifying when incorporated into weapon design, will yet light our cities and provide power for our factories, while research work done on such items as vehicles, textiles, or electronics can clearly not be classified as specifically either military or civilian. The same is true of developments in light alloys and of many other advances in metallurgy. In peace time new developments in food preservation and packaging may merely improve the standard of living, but in time of war, they could conceivably make the difference between survival and defeat.[20]

The argument was also made that all scientific advancement is based upon continuing "pure" research. Without the work of independent scientists devoted to the disinterested acquisition of new scientific knowledge neither new industrial developments nor weapons systems would be forthcoming.

The Defence Research Board thus gradually developed a dual role, becoming both an advisory body to the military establishment and an operating body actively involved in research.

On the operations side, seven defence research establishments were maintained by the Board. The Board's annual report briefly describes the research projects of each centre for the year under review, but the technical language used often offers little enlightenment to the lay reader. In the 1973 report, a list of research activities relating to military applications of lasers includes the following point as one of the year's achievements in the field: "Operation of a CO flame laser (burning CS_2, 0_2, and N_20) at a continuous power level of 4.5W, with a chemical efficiency corresponding to a 2% conversion of the available chemical energy to laser radiation." One can only assume that, from the point of view of the defence researcher, that is good news.

Nevertheless, the reports do reveal a wide range of research activities. In Dartmouth, Nova Scotia, the Defence Research Establishment Atlantic conducts major research programs in the field of underwater acoustics, analysing major underwater noise, such as may be associated with ice in northern waters, which might interfere with military operations, and hydrodynamics, developing new designs for surface ships and hydrofoil craft.

The program of the Defence Research Establishment Valcartier, at Valcartier, Quebec, includes laser research and the development of a Spinning Tubular Projectile (STUP), a new style of ammunition suitable for a variety of guns. *Ad hoc* tests of armor penetration were said to be "encouraging" because it was found that "a full-caliber STUP produced a large hole and removed a large volume of material from the target to enhance lethality." In other words a STUP bullet outperforms conventional ammunition in inflicting damage. Its use as a practice round for the 105 mm tank gun is being considered since the STUP is particularly suitable for practice exercises because a technique for controlling the trajectory makes it possible also to control range. The same feature interests military planners in that it also enables firing at high velocity yet short range. The 1973 report says that other applications of STUP, such as 20-30 mm ground-to-air and small arms ammunition, are also being considered and manufacturers have already examined the design for mass production.

The Defence Research Analysis Establishment in Ottawa operates, for the Department of National Defence, a General Analysis Division (GAD) and an Operational Research Division (ORD). The GAD conducts strategic analysis, sociological and economic analysis, logistics analysis, manpower analysis, and mathematics and statistics. The ORD provides operational research and analysis concerning the military functions and activities of the Department. It is concerned primarily with force planning, equipping, and operating. One specific interest is the Air Defence Command's surveillance in support of Canadian sovereignty and the ORD is studying the identification of aircraft entering Canadian airspace and, in particular, syas the Board, the intercept capability of aircraft deployed in the surveillance role.

The Board describes the objectives of the Defence and Civil Institute of Environmental Medicine as: (1) to expand the knowledge of the characteristics, capabilities, and limitations of man in hostile environments; (2) to study the human problems inherent in engineering systems; and (3) to apply this knowledge to effective design and development of man/machine systems for use in adverse environments, and to the effective education and clinical evaluation of military and civilian personnel. Equipment and physiological problems associated with living in the Arctic are a major concern.

The Defence Research Establishment Pacific at Esquimalt, British Columbia, also conducts acoustics research, along with research in the fields of electromagnetics, fluid dynamics and material engineering.

The most controversial research has been carried out in the two remaining centres, the Defence Research Establishment Ottawa (DREO) and the Defence Research Establishment Suffield (DRES) near Ralston, Alberta. Canadian research relating to chemical and biological warfare (CBW) has periodically become a subject of public concern due to suspicions and charges that Canada was participating in the development of chemical and biological weapons. The federal government has always insisted that its CBW research is concerned exclusively with the development of an effective system of defence against a CBW attack, and while it is probable that defence has become the main thrust of the research, distinctions between military defence and offence are more than a little obscure. The development of an effective defence presupposes an offensive capability and there is evidence to suggest that Canadian research has not ignored the offensive implications of some of its CBW work.

The Defence Research Establishment Ottawa has for more than thirty years been the main Canadian CBW research centre. The DRB yearbook describes the work as a "chemical defence program" which includes applied research on physical protection and on the detection and decontamination of chemical agents. An experimental model of an automatic detector and alarm device for liquid chemical warfare agents has been developed, as has a kit to detect and identify minute traces of chemical agents in the atmosphere. Work is being done on improving equipment for respiratory protection and several NATO countries are said to have shown interest in buying protective clothing and equipment developed by Canadian researchers.

While defence against CBW attack obviously requires effective protective clothing and equipment, it is also true that no military force could contemplate the offensive use of CBW agents if it did not possess an effective defence to protect its own troops that would be called on to follow up the attack. The development of these protective devices has over the years required extensive field trials as well as the development of techniques for distributing actual CBW agents or simulants. As a result, even though the Board points to the protective devices its research has developed, the fact is that the process of creating an effective defence includes the development of an effective offence.

The field trials were carried out on a tract of 1000 square miles of prairie land near Ralston, Alberta. The site is part of the Defence Research Establishment Suffield and contains a self-sustaining compound of buildings, including electrical plant, airport, road system, and natural gas supply. The official function of DRES is to conduct "applied research on problems concerned with protection against biological, chemical and nuclear warfare." (Reports, however, refer only to chemical and nuclear research, not biological.) The late Dr. Brock Chisholm describes some of the field trials that have taken place:

> During the war, the method of testing was to clear large areas of prairie in the Canadian West and to stake out prairie dogs, chickens, pigs and other animals at various points, widely distributed throughout the area. The fatalities were extraordinary—almost unbelievable and with very small quantities of botulinus toxin being used.[22]

The nature of field trials has no doubt changed over the years, but Canada's tripartite arrangement with the United States and Britain to share research facilities and information places severe strains on the claim that the work conducted in more recent times was exclusively defensive.

In 1967, the man then in charge of Suffield, Archie Pennie, was asked how the tripartite pact works:

> There are regular meetings of scientific staff engaged in this particular line of work (CBW) in all three countries and there is free disclosure of information in all these areas. We also attempt to divide the work between laboratories, whether they be in Britain, the United States or here; wherever the work suits. You can understand that you need specialized facilities for this type of work. There are facilities in Canada which don't exist in Britain, and there are some in Britain that do not exist in the United States, so it makes good sense and some logicality to try and divide up the work.[23]

Asked if each country is "a specialist in a specific field," Pennie replied: "Yes, this is true. There are particular areas where we are better suited, as a result of staff or training facilities, to do certain aspects of this kind of work." As for the Canadian speciality, he said:

> We have a large establishment on the prairies at Suffield . . . There we have an open air laboratory. We have a tract of ground made up of a thousand square miles of territory. This

is very useful when one is contemplating or assessing the usefulness of candidate agents in this type of field.

He explained further that "the program is jointly operated in this particular testing area, so it may be a program of testing some type of agent or candidate agent which has arisen as a result of British or American development.

The testing in this case is not of protective equipment but of the "usefulness" of a particular CBW agent, and the obvious implication seems to be that Canada specializes in testing CBW weapons devised by the United States and Britain. Hence Suffield's crucial 1000 square miles. The program, as described by Mr. Pennie, seems to have gone well beyond "defensive purposes" and it is not at all unreasonable to conclude that through such co-operation with the United States and the "free disclosure of information in all these areas," Canada actually contributed to American development and stockpiling of CBW agents, some of which were used in Indo-China.

Canada has signed the 1925 Geneva Convention banning chemical and bacteriological warfare, which is why DRB officials have always been very quick to point out that all Canadian CBW research is defensive, designed not to develop CBW but to develop a defence against it. But the Canadian commitment to share the results of her research with the Americans puts the claim, as we have suggested, in some doubt. The American journalist, Seymour Hersh, wrote in a book on CBW that Suffield research papers are widely circulated in the United States CBW labs and "U.S. Chemical Corps officials have circulated papers from another microbiological research centre in Ottawa" (a reference to DREO). Hersh went on to say that:

> Suffield has become colossally important to the CBW people here in the last year. Ever since the uproar came out over tests within the United States (the summer of '69) its a known thing in Washington that Suffield has become the U.S. prime testing area now.[24]

But Archie Pennie gives further evidence that research at Suffield is not strictly "defensive:"

In the last fifteen years the public generally visualizes mass attacks of choking clouds that either kill you instantaneously or give you Bubonic Plague or what have you. It's swung away from that into the area of non-lethal incapacitating agent. If you look at the hot zones of the world, you're fighting wars not on well-defined battlefield areas. You're dealing with towns in between it; civil population, friendly forces mixed with enemy forces. So maybe the thing to do is shake the pepper in and sort out the good from the bad. At the end of six hours they have a splitting headache, but they're alright the next day.

He was asked if Canadian peace keeping forces were able to do this today:

Well, I wouldn't say we have all types of material on hand, but this is the philosophy that we have to maintain to be alert to the capabilities of this type of operation of chemical agents. . . . Traditionally, if you look at the Canadian role, it has been one of keeping peace in the Congo, in Cyprus. In the chemical operations side, maybe the thing to do is to have something that will clear up the main streets Saturday night by some incapacitating but non-lethal agent.

This suggestion that Canadian forces become a sort of mobile chemical Green Berets does not sound like the purely defensive research Suffield is supposed to be engaging in to protect our shores from intruding clouds.

There is also evidence that in addition to participating in the development of particular agents, Canadian research has come up with new and improved methods of distributing them. The 1972 annual report of the DRB describes some of the "training in chemical defence" undertaken at Suffield. In order to give realistic training against attack, we are told, the Armed Forces must be able to stage a simulated attack. For this reason, DRES has developed "a prototype to simulate the dispersal of agents from ground burst munitions" called the Ground Burst Chemical Simulator. Work is now under way to develop a radio control firing capability which would make it possible to plant these Ground Burst Chemical Simulators in advance, much in the same way as land mines are planted, and then fire them from some remote control centre. NATO countries, we are told, have shown "considerable interest" and "one foreign request has been received for a number of the simulators for test." It seems possible that this so-called testing device could easily become an offensive weapon in CBW when actual chemical agents are substituted for the simulated agents used in training models. A retired American Brigadier, General, J. H. Rothschild, writes in his book, *Tomorrow's Weapons*, that land mines are a prominent means of carrying out certain types of attacks in chemical warfare.[25]

The Suffield establishment has been staunchly defended by former Member of Parliament, Harold E. Winch (NDP, Vancouver East), who visited the site for three days to personally check on charges that Canada was contributing to CBW capabilities through research work at Suffield. In his unpublished report, Winch said:

> I did not find a solitary instance, in my estimation, where the research work at Suffield is being undertaken in any manner whatsoever that the findings could be used by Canada or any other country for the aggressive use of chemical or germ warfare. All studies are for the protection of Canadian Armed Forces and civilian population if the occasion should arise that they are subject to either form of attack.

Mr. Winch further concluded that the work at Suffield should be continued and has a value for Canada beyond the immediate defence implications:

> The research studies at Suffield on chemicals, germs and noise give them a knowledge which, in my estimation, is most useful to the Canadian economy. I give a number of examples:
>
> 1. A request came in from one of the major industries in Canada asking whether or not it was possible to give information as to what would happen if a tank car of ammonia exploded. How far would it spread? How far would it be carried by the atmosphere, according to the wind direction and speed? What would be the best way to contain it? Suffield was able to give some specific information on this matter.

2. Another major industry in Canada asked if they could be given any information relative to the effluent from their discharge stacks. How far would it carry according to certain weather conditions and how could it best be controlled? Suffield was able to give some advice on this matter.

3. Inquiries reach Suffield relative to pesticides and insecticides, particularly as regards carrying power by the wind— when it is to be used only on a certain type of crop but is carried by the wind some miles further and can therefore kill another type of crop. Advice from knowledge can be given on this also.

Diagram 2 in Appendix VII shows the percentage distribution of the Board's $50.894,000 (1973-1974) budget to each division and of defence establishments, the two involved directly in CBW research received about one-fifth of the DRB funds (although it is to be noted that these two establishments carry out research work in fields other than CBW as well). The table below, which compares amounts devoted to CBW research in six Western countries, says that in 1971 Canada's direct expenditures on CBW research were $1.9 million, representing 2.4 per cent of all military research and development carried out in the country during that year. (If, by the way, $1.9 million represents 2.4 per cent of the total spent on military research and development, then the figure for the total is about $80 million for 1971—which is, as we have argued, a very conservative figure.)

Chemical and Biological Research and Development in Six Western European and North American Countries

	Year	Funding for CBBR&D	Persons working on program	% of total military R&D devoted to CBR&D
Canada	1971	$1.9 million	120	2.4%
Netherlands	1970	1.3	140	9.3
Sweden	1971	1.6	110	1.9
United Kingdom	1971	8.4	1250	1.3
United States	1971	6.0	5700	0.7
West Germany	1969	1.0	100	6.4

In April 1974 the minister of defence announced that all field trials in CBW defence research had been completed and that the Suffield establishment was being phased out in preparation for a 1977 closing. The minister said the Defence Research Establishment Ottawa would continue with the same kind of CBW research that had been carried out there since World War II and that all trials would be carried out in the laboratory. Earlier the minister had announced that a new $11.5 million defence research laboratory was to be established in his Winnipeg constituency. The new Winnipeg defence research establishment is eventually to have a staff of 70 scientists and an annual $6 million operating budget.

The Board's emphasis on the commercial implications of its work makes the research to production process an important one. If research efforts are to be translated into commercial enterprises, a way must be found to equitably make the findings of the researcher, funded by public moneys, available to the private producer.

The Board's stated policy is to leave, as much as possible, fundamental or pure research to the universities. This is not to say, however, that such research is simply left to chance. The Board has an interest in seeing particular kinds of research projects carried out at the universities and operates a program of almost $4 million in grants to see that the work gets done. (See Appendix III for distribution of funds.) The basic objectives of the grants program, as described by the Board, are "to acquire new scientific knowledge with potential for application to the solution of technical defence problems; to develop and support in the community an interest in defence science, to contribute to the long-term maintenance of a Canadian defence research capability."

The scientific staff of the DRB monitor these research projects and others in order to identify any possible military application. The Board's own research establishments are devoted to just that, to applying scientific advances to military technology. This process leads to what they call a "bread board model"—a kind of prototype of a military product developed by the Board's laboratories— which is then demonstrated to the Canadian Armed Forces as well as to foreign forces. If any defence department expresses an interest in procuring such a commodity, the DRB turns the bread board model over to a private firm for further development and, hopefully, production for a customer.

Since this development stage is still an economically risky one, with no firm orders yet obtained, the Board operates a "Defence Industrial Research Program" (see Appendix VI) to help the company along. The Program was established in 1961 to "stimulate an increase in the level of scientific and technological competence of the Canadian defence industry." For the 1973-1974 fiscal year, about $3,800,000 was spent on the Program, divided into the following fields:

Aeronautics	13.5%
Electrical Power Sources	3.0
Electronics	53.5
Aircraft propulsion	20.4
Mechanics and weapons	3.1
Total	100.0%

To decide which firm ultimately receives the "bread board model" for development and production and, consequently, profit, industries are canvassed to find firms with particular expertise in the appropriate area. Canadian Westinghouse, De Havilland, and Computing Devices of Canada are three firms mentioned by a DRB official as having a close working relationship with the Board; the president of Canadian Westinghouse Limited also happens to be a member of the Defence Research Board.

The implied conflict of interest in such relationships was raised as an issue, involving a different case, by Ed Broadbent, M.P. On January 27, 1970, Mr. Broadbent asked a question in the House of Commons concerning a conflict of interest involving Mr. J. B. Houlding, who was at the time both president of RCA Victor of Canada and a member of the DRB. In the period 1962-1970, RCA had received 493 contracts from the Department of National Defence and Mr. Broadbent asked if the minister would investigate this apparent conflict of interest. Leo Cadieux, the Minister of Defence at the time, replied simply that "technically speaking the contracts referred to here were not given by the Defence Research Board."[27] The next day, Mr. Broadbent raised the question again and this time Mr. Cadieux gave the following reply:

I believe it would be useful to indicate to the House that the terms of reference of the Defence Research Board designate representatives from industry, universities and other research interests in Canada as possible members of the Board. The case in point is a temporary assignment. I can reassure my Hon. friend by telling him that the Defence Research Board has no specific responsibility for directing purchasing for the government.[28]

As of April 1, 1974, the Defence Research Board was relieved of its operations function and restricted to an advisory-evaluation role, and all research operations were absorbed by the Defence Department. The changes were based on recommendations by a management review group which had studied the entire working structure of the Department of National Defence and concluded that a single body should not both advise the minister and assume the responsibility for carrying out resulting operations. The operations budget of the DRB, therefore, became a part of the Departmental budget and some 2000 staff members became employees of the Department.

The changes will have important repercussions for the Board itself, but, according to a statement issued by the Department, will have "little or no impact on the internal organization of the individual defence research establishments." It can be assumed that research carried out will continue as before but absorption by the Department of National Defence may make the actual amounts spent on defence research even more difficult to trace.

In recent years, the United States Department of Defence has become an even more important source of funds for research in Canadian institutions than is the Defence Research Board of Canada. Figures supplied by the Pentagon show that in 1969 the Pentagon spent $6,816,802 on defence research in Canadian institutions.[29] But figures supplied by Senator William Fullbright show $9,760,340 being spent in Canada during that year. What makes the Fullbright figures even more revealing is the fact that they exclude most of $5,831,000 paid to the Canadian Commercial Corporation—the latter figure, however, was included in the Pentagon figures. In other words, the Pentagon seems to have spent a minimum of about $14 million on defence research in Canadian institutions in 1969. (*How to Make a Killing*, Appendix IV, reproduces pages showing the details of grants by the Pentagon to individual institutions in Canada.)

The following statement, which comprises part of the conditions under which the grants are received, speaks for itself:

The abiding concern of the Air Force Office of Scientific Research is that granted funds are always used to achieve a maximum contribution to the knowledge essential to the continued superiority of the Air Force operational capability, and it is assumed that grantees and principal investigators will always direct their efforts to this end.

Notes

1 *House of Commons Debates*, January 27, 1970.

2 *Economic and Social Consequences of the Arms Race and of Military Expenditures*, Report of the Secretary-General (New York: A United Nations Publication, 1972), p. 15.

3 *1973 Yearbook of World Armaments and Disarmament.*

4 Max Wilde, *Rand Daily Mail*, April 19, 1974.

5 *Review '73*, Defence Research Board Annual Report, p. 11.

6 Ibid.

7 Max Wilde, *Rand Daily Mail*, April 19, 1974.

8 *SIPRI Yearbook, 1969/70*; pp. 288ff.

9 William Cobban, "Dealing Out Death Discreetly: The Traffic in Canadian Arms," *Saturday Night*, November 1971.

10 *House of Commons Debates*, October 30, 1969.

11 *House of Commons Debates*, March 7, 1973.

12 *1972 Yearbook of World Armaments and Disarmament.*

13 Standing Committee on Finance, Trade and Economic Affairs, *Proceedings*, April 1, 1969.

14 *The Defence Research Board: The First Twenty-five Years*, p. 12.

15 M. J. Goodspeed, *A History of the Defence Research Board of Canada* (Ottawa: Queen's Printer, 1958), p. 8.

16 Ibid.

17 *DRB: The First 25 Years*, p. 11.

18 Goodspeed, *op. cit.*, p. 10.

19 Ibid., p. 26.

20 Ibid., p. 25.

21 *DRB Review 1972*, pp. 27-28.

[22] John Cookson and Judith Nottingham, *A Survey of Chemical and Biological Warfare* (New York: Monthly Review Press, 1969), p. 102.

[23] The December 1969 issue of *Last Post* reports Mr Pennie's comments in some detail.

[24] Seymoor M. Hersh, *Chemical and Biological Warfare: America's Hidden Arsenal* (Bobbs-Merill Co., 1968), pp. 293-294.

[25] J. H. Rothschild, *Tomorrow's Weapons.*

[26] "The Problem of Chemical and Biological Warfare", Vol. II, *CB Weapons Today*, The Stockholm International Pease Research Institute: (New York: Humanities Press, 1973).

[27] *House of Commons Debates*, January 27, 1970.

[28] *House of Commons Debates*, January 28, 1970.

[29] These and the following figures taken from *How to Make a Killing.*

5   From Gun-running to Peace-making

It seems doubtful whether civilization can stand another
major war, and it is at least thinkable that the way out lies
through non-violence.

George Orwell

Canadian arms merchants insist, of course, that emotive terms like
"gun-runners" or "merchants of death" have little to do with the
export of olive-green underwear or telephone equipment—even if
they do happen to be for "field" use. Indeed, by the standards of a
Krupp, this country's defence industry appears almost genteel.

Like any arms industry worthy of the name, the Canadian war
business maintains a "supply capability" in such overtly military
items as bombs, weapons and ammunition, (in 1973, for example,
items in all these categories were sold to the United States through
the Canadian Commercial Corporation for shipment to Vietnam)
but its mainstay is neither bombs nor guns but noncommital items
such as airframes, component parts for various types of machinery,
and electronic equipment. There is, they argue, very little gun-
running—only straight-forward business deals to supply long-
standing allies or sister corporations with "sophisticated communications equipment" and other similarly innocuous-sounding commodities.

Furthermore, defence industry apologists point out, it is a matter of security. Our way of life depends ultimately on our ability to
protect it, through military preparedness, from external attack, and
if we make a little profit in the process, well, that's only good
business from which all Canadians benefit. Defence production
breeds technical sophistication, and even bleeding hearts must
agree that no modern trading nation can be without technical sophistication. Besides, if we didn't supply foreign markets, some-

body else would, so it might as well be Canadian industry that gets the orders.

But Canada's promotion of a growing arms industry has gone beyond well-meaning efforts to mitigate the economic costs of maintaining national security. Armaments may be considered a "necessary" evil that any realistic and prudent nation will keep on hand, but Canada has gone out of its way to exploit and trade on the human weakness that gives in to such "necessity." In an imperfect world men will continue to submit, in varying degrees, to the use and treat of violence as a "necessary" condition of national life, but the measure of moral maturity for men and political maturity for governments is still to be found in the extent to which they struggle against this "necessity." Canada, by its efforts to build a thriving defence industry, has ceased to struggle against "necessity"—against the war system—and has chosen instead to make as much money as possible out of that system, thereby creating for itself a growing economic stake in the use of armaments to solve political problems, even though official foreign policy deplores "violent solutions."

As the result of more than three decades of careful nurture, the production of military commodities has become progressively more important to the Canadian economy, both in the development of industrial technology and trade performance. Canadians may not yet be in the relentless grip of an overpowering military/industrial complex, but the policies of successive governments have been pushing steadily in that direction.

The process really began with the Mackenzie King government's rearmament program in the 1930s. Because the government was anxious to reduce its reliance upon foreign sources for arming and equipping its forces, a policy of domestic production was established and important steps were taken to begin the building of an indigenous defence industry. World War II gave the fledgling industry a major boost and the manufacture of war goods became a central part of Canada's contribution to the war effort (two-thirds of Canadian production during the war was exported and the resulting economic benefits did not go unnoticed).

Under cover of the war effort, Canada entered into co-operative production arrangements with her allies, principally the United States, and Canadian policy shifted from self-sufficiency to shared production. The principle was established by the Liberals at Hyde Park in 1941 and given institutional form by the Conservatives in

1958 when the Canada/United States Defence Production Sharing arrangements were adopted. In the process, Canadian interest in defence production shifted from assured supply to economic opportunity and the federal government, in an effort to establish a defence industry capable of competing in international markets, became a major benefactor of firms in the war business. Assistance was, and is, provided in the form of liaison with foreign buyers and direct financial aid. Through the Defence Industry Productivity Program (about $40 million per year), the Defence Research Board (about $50 million per year), Pentagon-funded research in Canadian institutions (perhaps $14 million per year), and general "incentives" to industry, the annual public expenditure on military research and development in Canada came to be measured not in tens of millions of dollars but in hundreds of millions.

Though it is promoted for economic reasons, the economic consequences of defence production are by no means entirely beneficial. Defence production sharing has generated additional pressures for a North American common market in raw materials (the 1950 principles said that "the two countries shall, as it becomes necessary, institute co-ordinated controls over the distribution of scarce raw materials and supplies"): it has encouraged the domination of the Canadian industry by its American counterpart (the federal Minister of Industry, Trade and Commerce admitted as much when he announced intentions to place De Havilland and Canadair in Canadian ownership, saying that the companies had no independent authority to make decisions or to control their own growth and development); and the industry's extensive reliance upon United States procurement policies has made it directly vulnerable to decisions made in the Pentagon—all these factors impair independent economic planning in Canada and submerge Canadian economic interest in favour of the continental interest.

Following World War II, it was argued that defence research was necessary to "be able to make the best possible equipment choices and to shape the most effective defence policies," but the commercialization of defence research—by which product marketability became the measure of success—and of the industry in general were seriously to undermine the basic objectives. The short-term commercial advantages of arms exports have resulted not in better Canadian defence policies but in continental defence policies. Defence production sharing is part and parcel of

NORAD and NATO—that, at least, was the opinion of Prime Minister Pearson—and participation in these two alliances commit Canada to a role in the game of nuclear deterrance, a role that can realistically only be played as an addendum to American super-power diplomacy.

Canadian exports of defence products beyond the shores of North America tend, because of shared equipment models, to follow American exports, and defence research contributes to the momentum of the runaway arms race.

Canada's arms business is without redeeming virtues. It serves no positive good—save the short-term commercial advantage of the direct participants. In the meantime both morality and long-term self-interest are violated. But opposition to arms exports and defence production sharing obviously involves more than declarations of moral outrage at merchants of death. The implications, of which the necessary economic adjustments may turn out to be the easiest to deal with, are largely unknown and bound to be far-reaching. Changeovers from military to non-military production are not impossible to achieve, but the military/political adjustments could be the more difficult to accept.

The substantial dismantling of a defence industry implies, in fact, a partial rejection of militarism as the final means to state security, and no country is likely to tolerate that without concrete evidence that other forms of defence are available and practical. There is the mistaken impression abroad that non-military defence consists simply of doing nothing. In fact, a defence system premised on the principle of non-violence requires as much training, research, and overall preparedness as does military defence. A population that is neither schooled in non-violence nor pacifist by moral persuasion will obviously have little confidence in a non-military defence system if there are no steps taken to make the system understood. Similarly, no population is likely to welcome the dismantling of its defence industry if it continues to believe that effective defence depends ultimately upon military prowess.

In the nuclear age, military might offers little security. The survival of a nation, both physically and culturally, has become much more probable by way of passive resistance than by warfare. It is a style of defence that has to date held little attraction for the nation state, but which will require serious research if opposition to the international trade in the instruments of war is ever to go beyond pious rhetoric.

For the government's part, no one can expect a single dramatic switch from a system of military defence to a system of nonviolent civilian defence, but it is reasonable to expect that it devote at least as much energy to the search for nonviolent alternatives as it does to the development and sales of instruments of violence. Changes must realistically occur in stages, and the first, and absolutely essential, of these is the renunciation of all participation in the international trade in arms. The implications of even this minimum move would be substantial and should not be dismissed lightly. The loss of export sales would mean the loss of jobs and would require efforts to retool affected industries for civilian production. Furthermore, the cost of equiping Canadian forces would be drastically increased. But that could turn out to be a blessing in disguise, providing a convincing incentive to re-examine equipment needs and to investigate alternatives. For the most part, alternatives to military defence have not been highly developed, but the following account demonstrates that serious defence planners have at least contemplated non-violence as a tactic for national defence.

George F. Kennan, formerly a member of the American State Department planning staff, proposed in 1958 that Western Europe could be defended not exclusively by non-violent methods but by means that would give wide scope to such methods. Kennan's proposal comes out of the context of the Cold War and assumes that the Soviet Union has aggressive designs on Western Europe:

> If the armed forces of the United States and Britain were not present on the continent, the problem of defence for the continental nations would be primarily one of the internal health and discipline of the respective national societies and of the manner in which they were organized to prevent the conquest and subjugation of their national life by unscrupulous and foreign-inspired minorities in their midst. What they need is a strategic doctrine addressed to this reality. Under such a doctrine, armed forces would indeed be needed; but I would suggest that as a general rule these forces might better be para-military ones, of a territorial-militia type, somewhat

on the Swiss example, rather than regular military units on the World Warr II pattern . . . .The training of such forces ought to be such as to prepare them not only to offer whatever overt resistance might be possible to a foreign invader but also to constitute the core of a civil resistance movement on any territory that might be over-run by the enemy; and every forethought should be exercised to facilitate their assumption and execution of this role in the case of necessity. For this reason they need not, and should not, be burdened with heavy equipment, or elaborate supply requirements, and this means—and it is no small advantage—that they could be maintained at a small fraction of the cost per unit of the present conventional (military) establishments.

It is a strategy to bring the defence of the country essentially to the population itself. For the concept of the "ring of steel" at the frontier, Kennan substitutes the concept of a citizen army "honeycombing" the entire country.

The purpose would be to place the country in a position where it could face the Kremlin and say to it: "Look here, you may be able to overrun us, if you are unwise enough to attempt it, but you will have small profit from it; we are in a position to assure that not a single Communist or other person likely to perform your political business will be available to you for this purpose. . . . Your stay among us will not be a happy one. . . . "

Any nation able to say this, believes Kennan, "will have little need for foreign garrisons to assure its immunity from Soviet attack." Preparations of such a nature would become a powerful nonnuclear and only partially military deterrent.

In an imperfect world, the elimination of conflict may well remain a fond hope, but the curbing of warfare is not only a reasonable hope but the responsibility of every nation claiming to work towards a world of peace. But in a world of political realities, violence will not be rejected on faith. It will be rejected only when alternatives are shown to have at least as much chance for success. All one can ask is that Canadian diplomatic endeavour be on the side that searches for alternatives, rather than on the side that cynically exploits the present system of violence and counter-violence for short-term economic benefit.

Disarmament and non-violence represent a measure of political and diplomatic maturity devoutly to be wished, but first we will have to grow out of the political adolescence that places such a narrow interpretation on self-interest as to permit us, while speaking piously of favouring non-violent solutions, to run guns for profit.

Notes

1 W. R. Miller cites Kennan's proposal in a discussion of nonviolent national defence in his book, *Nonviolence: A Christian Interpretation* (New York: Schocken Books, 1966).

Appendix I

Sample pages from *Canadian Defence Products*, a detailed catalogue of the products of the Canadian defence industry.

Tilt-wing Aircraft (CL-84)

The CL-84 is being developed as a highly versatile vehicle with the potential of fulfilling a wide variety of roles that otherwise require the use of both fixed and rotary-wing aircraft. Its military applications are expected to comprise combat support, personnel and cargo transport, reconnaissance, search and rescue, helicopter escort, and communications, from both land bases and aircraft carriers.

Performance flexibility of this order is made possible by the novel "tilt-wing" design of the CL-84 which allows the aircraft to take off vertically and hover like a helicopter, yet fly forward like an airplane at speeds up to 350 mph (563 km/hr). With the wing tilted between the vertical and horizontal, the CL-84 has impressive performance and manoeuvrability at very low speeds and outstanding short take-off and landing (STOL) capabilities.

Although this aircraft is designed for vertical, STOL, and fixed-wing flight, the pilot's primary cockpit controls consist of the standard aeroplane rudder pedals, stick, and single throttle (power lever) which incorporates the wing-tilt switch. (There is no requirement for a collective pitch lever). Because of this simplicity, an experienced pilot will be able to devote virtually his full attention to his operational task rather than to flying the aircraft.

Commercial developments of the Canadair CL-84 would substantially reduce total travel time for passenger transportation between city-centers 100 to 500 miles (161 to 805 km) apart. Also, because such aircraft can operate independent of normal runways, they have considerable potential for survey, exploration and general transport work in undeveloped areas.

Evaluation models for the Canadian Armed Forces are now in production at Canadair.

CF-5/NF-5.—Tactical Support Fighter

A total of 220 CF-5/NF-5 tactical fighter aircraft have been delivered to the Canadian Armed Forces and the Royal Netherlands Air Force. The Canadian (CF-5) and Netherlands (NF-5) versions are similar in most respects and were developed from the Northrop F-5. Production at Canadair's Montreal plant is under a license arrangement through the Canadian Government with the Northrop Corporation.

CF-5/NF-5s incorporate many improvements over the basic F-5 model including a stepped-up performance resulting from the increased power available from the General Electric J.85-15 engines. Each engine produces 4,300 lb. (1950 kg) thrust for an engine weight of only 615 lb. (279 kg). The NF-5 is equipped with manoeuvring flaps which provide outstanding handling qualities at high speeds and the CF-5 has an alternative camera equipped nose section as a rapid change item. These are examples of the more important improvements.

The F-5 was designed for tactical support, interdiction and interceptor roles and to these, the CF-5 has added both high and low level photo reconnaissance capabilities and many other important operational features.

The CF-5 combined the capabilities and performance normally associated with larger and more complex aircraft with rugged strength necessary for the low level tactical role and for operating from semi-prepared forward air strips. With a low operating cost and many ease-of-maintenance and safety features, the CF-5 is a weapon system ideally suited to the constantly changing requirements of an increasingly complex cost and defence environment.

Weapon Release Computer Set (AN/ASQ-91)

Manufactured in Canada by Litton Systems (Canada) Limited, the AN/ASQ-91 Weapon Release Computer Set is an analog weapon delivery system designed to enhance the combat effectiveness of the McDonnell F-4D/E aircraft. Compatibility of the Weapon Release Computer Set with the LN-12A Inertial Navigation Set used in the F-4C aircraft may be achieved through substitution of the LN-12D Output Signal Distribution Unit. The Weapon Release Computer Set provides range calculations and automatic weapons release signals for the laydown, dive-laydown, dive-toss and off-set bombing modes of operation. Steering signals and range-to-target information are supplies for use in the target-finding and off-set bombing modes. Manoeuvre commands and the release signal are provided for successful delivery of the AGM-45 missile. Either low-drag or high-drag bombs may be used through proper adjustment of the weapons release computer control panel drag coefficient control. Maximum use of F-4D/E aircraft inertial navigation set output signals and electronic components and mode-sharing of weapons release computer set components has achieved substantial reductions in size, weight, and cost of the equipment.

The Litton computer set consists of:
● The Ballistic Computer unit which contains all of the analog circuitry

required to solve the bombing problem for each mode of computer set operation;

- The Cursor Control Panel which incorporates two thumbwheel controls for adjusting the position of the long-track and cross-track cursors on the radar screen during the target finding and off-set bombing modes;
- The Weapons Release Computer Control Panel which contains controls and switches for mode selection, built-in test operation, and insertion of various range, altitude, time and ballistic information.

Gun Alignment and Control System

Recent efforts to improve the effectiveness of field artillery have focussed on increased sophistication in command and control functions at the battery and higher levels, notably through the use of fire control computers and observation post—command post data links. Canadian Armed Forces studies have shown that streamlining of the battery command post-to-gun control function yields a high relative payoff in response time reduction versus development effort. The Gun Alignment and Control System (GACS) being developed for the Canadian Armed Forces by Aviation Electric Limited arises from a new alignment philosophy proposed by the Canadian Forces and tested for feasibility by Defence Research Establishment Valcartier.

GACS is designed to provide the means for rapidly and accurately determining and communicating data required to orient each weapon in a fire unit, to provide a link for command and control of the weapons, and to allow rapid reversion to existing fire control procedures in the case of a malfunction. The system has three major components: a reference unit (RU), gun unit (GU) and command post unit (CPU), the latter two being joined by a Command and Control Link (CCL). The RU provides continuous (once per second) optically-coded orientation information simultaneously for all guns in a fire unit. Each GU receives the optical orientation information from the RU and displays it numerically, or combines it input of fire control data and provides an operator's display and loop verification to ensure error-free data transmission. The CCL may be either radio or wire line.

Method of Alignment

The RU, mounted on a standard military tripod, is oriented on grid north by any conventional means (gyro orienter, for example). Once oriented it transmits optically-coded orientation information in the infra-red region by means of an omni-directional Xenon flasher and a rotating laser diode linked to a shaft encoder. As the laser rotates (1 cycle/second), the Xenon flasher pulses once for every 40 mils of arc and gives a double pulse when the laser beam passes through the south direction.

The infra-red receiver portion of each GU is mounted on the gunsight. It senses the double Xenon pulse and starts a clock (local oscillator) which is "driven" by the periodic single Xenon pulses. Sensing of the laser beam by the IR receiver stops the clock and logic circuits linked to the interpolating oscillator express the elapsed time as a measure of the angle "R", rounding off to the nearest mil. This angle can be displayed by itself or combined automatically with data transmitted from the CPU to give the angle "S". The layer applies the angle S to the gunsight and lays on the RU to engage the specified target.

Advantage of GACS

The system yields a significant improvement in time into action by providing for immediate and simultaneous orientation of all guns in a fire unit. Current procedures require approximately five minutes for a troop of four guns under ideal conditions and can take much longer. With GACS all guns in the range of and inter-visible with the RU can be in action within one minute under a wide range of conditions.

Once-per-second generation of orientation data allows movement of guns on the position while firing and rapid return to action after any gun malfunction.

Internal Immersion Lenses for Submersibles

Leitz Canada has developed a family of fully water-corrected lenses for various film formats from 16 mm to 70 mm using a front dome which is in direct contact with sea water. This patented system allows the correction of these lenses to the same degree of performance in water as is now obtainable in aerial lenses.

When deep-sea photography is required, cameras are usually mounted on rigs or on the outside of submersibles, which limits the photographic mission by the film capacity of the camera system. It was, therefore, deemed desirable to develop a new water-corrected lens system which would permit the use of cameras inside a submersible. The lens shown on this data sheet describes this immersion system.

As wide-angle coverage should not interfere with continuous sampling alarms issued to units and visual observation, a lens system with an external entrance pupil was selected, therefore keeping the lens diameter small and maintaining the maximum field of view of the operator. To achieve the necessary correction and angular coverage, the lens has been designed as an immersion lens, that is to say, the space between the inner surface of the plano viewing port and the front surface of the lens is filled with a liquid medium of optical properties identical with, or similar to, the outside water environment. Various methods of attaching the lens to the port-hole, either permanently or temporarily, are possible and the user may select his own preference. One method would be to cement a small mounting cylinder against the port-hole and attach the lens by means of a bayonet ring, another would be to use a simple rubber suction cup against the window.

Air Cushion Vehicles

To meet the demand for effective, economical transportation, particularly in those areas not easily accessible, including Arctic regions, Bell Aerospace Canada has developed a heavy-haul air cushion vehicle.

This ACV is capable of handling a 22.580 kg (50,000 lb.) payload on a rugged flatbed structure of welded aluminum extrusions. The transmission systems, lift fans, propellors and skirt elements have been proven in over 100,000 hours of hover-craft operation. It is powered by two 1,300-shaft-horsepower ST-6 "Twin Pac" power plants built by United Aircraft of Canada Ltd., having multi-fuel capability and cold-weather starting features which have been proven during more than five million operating hours.

The design of the vehicle permits economic production and ensures that operating costs will be approximately one-quarter that of present heavy-lift helicopters. The concept of modular construction, where no piece is greater than 12 m x 2.4 m x .91 m (40 x 8 x 3 ft.), permits rapid assembly or disassembly for transportation by road, rail and air and operation on the new site. The design also features minimal maintenance and crew training. The flatbed design caters to a variety of super-structures and therefore allows transformation to many different types of craft and of course uses. Present potential uses include Coast-Guard support roles, mass-transit ferry; mining, oil and construction industries support.

Specifications

Length: 19.8 m (65 ft.)
Beam: 11.2 m (37 ft.)
Height (on cusion): 6.7 m (22 ft.)
Skirt Height: 1.2 m (4 ft.)
Weight, max. gross: 40,000 kg (88,000 lb.)
Fuel capacity: 9,000 litres (1,980 Imperial)
Speed (calm water, typical pay load): 45 knots

Impact Extrusion Components

One of Canada's largest manufacturers of aluminum impact extrusions is General Impact Extrusions (Manufacturing) Ltd., Toronto, Ontario. This Company specializes in the impact extrusion of metals, primarily aluminum. Its fabrication capabilities include a wide variety of precision defence components, collapsible tubes, vials, mailing containers, aerosol cans and other lithographed parts for the packaging industry; and various components for the automotive, appliance, electronic and atomic fields.

General Impact Extrusions have, for many years, produced parts and components for defence applications. Items produced include pistons, ammunition shells, missile parts, flare casings, rocket components, tail fin assemblies, and many other precision cold forgings.

Impact extrusion is a process of cold forming metals under high pressures. This method is a most efficient way to produce cans, shells and other hollow shapes. It is a high output process ideally suited to satisfy not only the precision military requirements, but also the high volume requirements of the packaging, automotive and electronic industries. Press capabilities for impacts are up to 15.24 cm (6 in.) diameter in lengths of up to 63.5 cm (25 in.) and for precision forward extrusions up to 6.4 cm (2.5 in.) diameter in lengths of up to 3.04 m (10 ft.) maximum.

G.I.E. production facilities include 24 extrusion presses and well over 160 miscellaneous machine tools, draw presses, coining presses, lathes, automatic chuckers, multispindle chuckers, automatic drills, automatic screw machines, drill presses and special purpose machines to handle components from 3.175 mm (¼ in.) to 177.8 mm (7 in.) diameter in lengths of up to (25 in.)

Heat treating, annealing, anodizing and alodining facilities are also available to ensure that the level of quality control demanded by the Company is, in fact, maintained.

A competent engineering staff is available for your assistance. Engineering services include alloys selection, strength and performance specifications, part designs, and production engineering. Other services include small lot production for pre-production testing, evaluation and testing of physical properties and performance.

Mine Anti-personnel Non-metallic C3A1 (M25)

These mines were developed by the Canadian Army and have been accepted as standard by ABC countries. The C3A1 version contains an sisting of the body assembly; 5 x 7.5 cm (2 in. diameter by 3 in. long) with a weight of 57 gm (2 oz); and the charge assembly, 3.8 x 5.6 cm (1.5 in. long by 2.2 in. diameter) with a weight of 28 gm (1 oz.). The total weight of the explosive is 9.45 gm.

The body assembly has a transit plug, which is removed after the body assembly has been emplaced and replaced by the charge assembly, fitted with a safety clip. Removal of the safety clip prepares the mine for function, under a load of 7.25—11.8 kg (16 to 26 lb.). As long as the safety clip remains in place, loads of extreme magnitude will not cause actuation.

The mines are coloured olive drab and are designed with integral camouflage material. Emplaced mines, after removal of the safety clip, are operationally undetectable with conventional electro-magnetic detection equipment. A detector ring can be fitted if this should be required, which makes the mine detectable by standard methods. This Anti-Personnel Mine is suitable for use in all classes of mine fields in primary or secondary roles. Examples of operational use would be to protect positions to prevent the lifting of Anti-Tank Mines and to deny terrain to attacking forces. The mine has been loaded by Canadian Arsenals Limited, Filling Division, with components supplied from various sources. The item is in volume production for the United Kingdom.

Mine Anti-personnel Non-metallic Practice C4A1

The mine is a practice version of the C3A1 (M25) H.E. mine.

The emplacement assembly and function of the practice mine is the same as for the H.E. version. On actuation, the mine produces a blue coloured smoke signal.

Identification of the components is made through the use of standard NATO colours. It is constructed of plastic materials and is reusable at least five times by replacement of the spotting charge and the re-cocking of the body assembly. This item has been in volume production for the Canadian Forces and the United Kingdom by Canadian Industries Limited and other contractors. Imitation inert and dummy versions of the C3A1 Anti-Personnel Mine have been manufactured and are available as required.

Appendix II

Companies in Canada receiving contracts from the United States Department of Defence, 1967-1972. (Reproduction of relevant pages from *How to Make a Killing*, by Project Anti-War of Montreal.)

1. Abex Industries (Canada) Ltd.
2. Aircraft Appliances and Equipment Ltd.
3. All Boro Metal Products Ltd.
4. Allen-Bradley Canada (AB)
5. Almax Ceramics Industries Limited (AC)
6. Aluminum Company of Canada Ltd.
7. Aluminum Foundry & Pattern Works Ltd.
8. American Gear Ltd.
9. Anaconda American Brass Ltd.
10. Anaconda Canada Limited
11. Andrew Corporation
12. A. S. M. Corp. Ltd.
13. Atco Industries Ltd. and Atco Research and Development Centre
14. Atlas Alloys Ltd.
15. Atlas Steels of Canada Ltd.
16. Aviation Electric Ltd.
17. Barringer Research Corp. Ltd.
18. Base Maintenance Ltd.
19. Beaconing Optical & Precision Materials Co. Ltd.
20. Beavers Dental Products Ltd.
21. Bell-Northern Research
22. Benco Television Ltd.
23. Berger Automotive Ltd.
24. Bituminous Sealing Corp. Ltd.
25. Block Lumber Ltd.
26. Borg-Warner Canada Ltd.
27. Bowmar Canada Ltd.
28. Bristol Aerospace Ltd.
29. Burlington Steel Division of Slater Steel Industries
30. C.A.E. Electronics Ltd.
31. C.A.E. Industries Ltd.
32. Canada Forgings Limited (Can. Forge)
33. Camden Refrigerating Terminal Ltd.
34. Canadair Ltd.

35. Canadian Acme Screw and Gear Ltd.
36. Canadian Admiral Corp. Ltd.
37. Canadian Aircraft Products Ltd.
38. Canadian Bronze Comapny Ltd.
39. Canadian Commercial Corp.
40. Canadian Flight Equipment Ltd.
41. Canadian General Electric Co. Ltd.
42. Canadian Industries Ltd.
43. Canadian Marconi Ltd.
44. Canadian Overseas Telecommunication Corp. Ltd.
45. Canadian Precision Devices Ltd.
46. Canada Pumps Ltd.
47. Canadian Research Institute
48. Canadian Safety Fuse Co. Ltd.
49. Canadian SKF Ltd. and (SKF) Ball & Roller Bearings
50. Canadian Westinghouse Ltd.
51. Canada Wire & Cable Ltd.
52. Cannon Electric (I.T.T.)
53. Canron Ltd.
54. Cercast Inc.
55. Chromasco Corporation Limited
56. Collins Radio Ltd.
57. Colt Industries (Canada) Ltd. Crucible Steel Division
58. Computing Devices of Canada Ltd.
59. Continental Motor Corp. of Canada Ltd.
60. Corbert Investment Ltd.
61. Courcellette Ltd.
62. Covington J. P. Corp. Ltd.
63. Cummins Eastern Ltd.
64. Cyberex Ltd.
65. Davidson Steel Co. Ltd.
66. Defense Research Board
67. De Havilland Aircraft of Canada Ltd.
68. Demers, Gordon, Baby Ltee. System Consultants
69. Desitron Co. Ltd.
70. Detroit Bolt & Nut Co. Ltd.
71. Diamond Construction Co. (1961) Ltd.
72. Dominion Aluminum Fabricating Ltd.
73. Dominion Foundries & Steel Ltd.
74. Dominion Road Machinery Co. Limited
75. Donald Ropes and Wire Cloth Ltd.
76. Dowty Equipment of Canada Ltd.
77. Dunlap Canada Ltd.
78. Dynamic Industries Inc.

79. Eastern Die Casting Inc.
80. Eastern Provincial Airways Ltd.
81. Edo (Canada) Limited
82. Eltra of Canada Ltd.
83. Enamel & Heating Products Limited
84. EF Tools Limited
85. English Electric Valve Ltd.
86. Engmark Ltd.
87. Erie Technological Products of Canada Ltd.
88. Esso International
89. Explosives Engineering Corp. Ltd.
90. Fabricated Steel Products (Windsor) Ltd.
91. Fag Bearings Ltd.
92. Farrar Electric Ltd.
93. Fathom Oceanology Ltd.
94. Federal Electric Corp. Ltd.
95. Ferranti-Packard Ltd.
96. Fisher Gauge (FG)
97. Flextrack-Nodwell Ltd.
98. Ford Motor Co. of Canada Ltd.
99. G. T. E. Automatic Electric Ltd.
100. Gabriel of Canada Ltd.
101. Garrett Manufacturing Ltd.
102. General Impact Extrusions Ltd.
103. General Metallic Parts Ltd.
104. General Precision Industries Ltd.
105. Golden Eagle of Canada Ltd.
106. Greening Donald Ltd.
107. Greg Gary International
108. Guildline Instruments Ltd.
109. H & S Construction Co. Ltd.
110. Hallmark Standards Ltd.
111. Harnischfeger Corp. of Canada Limited (P&H)
112. Hamilton Gear & Machine Co.
113. Hawker Siddeley Canada Ltd. Canadian Bridge Division
114. Headland Construction Co. Ltd.
115. Hermes Electronics Ltd.
116. Heroux Ltd.
117. Hickcok Electrical Instruments
118. Holland Hitch of Canada Ltd.
119. Frank W. Horner Limited (H) Pharmaceuticals (Operations)
120. Hovey and Associates Ltd.
121. IBM Canada Ltd.
122. Ingersol Machine & Tool Co. Ltd.

123. Industrial Components Corp. Ltd.
124. Industrial Wire & Cable Company
125. Inland Containers Ltd.
126. Instronics Ltd.
127. International Harvestor Co. (Canada) Ltd.
128. International Nickel Co. (Canada) Ltd.
129. I.T.T. Arctic Services Ltd.
130. I.T.T. Canada Ltd.
131. Irv. Ind. (FSF) Ltd.
132. Jacobson Bros. Ltd.
133. Jahn A. G. Ltd.
134. Jet Janitor Services Ltd.
135. Johns-Manville Sales Corp.
136. Kaar Electronics Corp.
137. Kaltenbach R. W. Corp.
138. Daman Corp.
139. KELK George Kelk Ltd. Electronics Electromechanics
140. Leigh Instruments Ltd.
141. Leitz, Ernst Canada Ltd.
142. Lindsay, J.M. Construction Ltd.
143. Litton Industries (Canada) Ltd.
144. Litton Systems (Canada) Ltd.
145. Lockes Electrical Ltd.
146. Lockheed Aircraft Ltd.
147. Lucas-Rotex Ltd.
148. Lumonics Research Ltd.
149. Magna Electronics Ltd.
150. Mansfield-Denman General Co. Lim. Industrial Products Division G-Tire
151. Maritime Aircraft Ltd.
152. Marsland Engineering Ltd.
153. Manasco Manufacturing Co. of Canada Ltd.
154. Miehle-Goss-Dexter (Canada) Ltd.
155. Microsystems International Ltd.
156. Mimik Limited Machine Tool-Tracer Controls
157. Moloney Electric Company of Canada Limited (M) Marketing Services
158. National Semiconductors Ltd.
159. Nelson Erection Co. Ltd.
160. Newland Painters & Decorators Ltd.
161. Noranda Metal Industries Ltd.
162. Nordair Ltd.
163. North American Rockwell Corp.
164. Northern Electric Co. Ltd.

165. Norton Research Corporation (Canada) Ltd.
166. Noseworthy, C. H. Ltd.
167. Novatronics of Canada Ltd.
168. O & W Electronics Ltd.
169. Oconto Electric Ltd.
170. Okanagan Helicopters Ltd.
171. Ontario Rubber Co. Ltd.
172. Ormont Drug & Chemical Co. Inc.
173. Osborne Electric Co. Ltd.
174. Otaco Ltd.
175. P & W. Aircraft Supplies Ltd.
176. Paint Craft Ltd.
177. Parelman H., Roofing Ltd.
178. Parkers Bros. Ltd.
179. Perfection Automotive Products (Windsor) Ltd.
180. Phillips Cables Ltd.

181. Picker Corp.
182. Pines R. H. Corp.
183. Pinsent Construction Co. Ltd.
184. Pirelli Canada Ltd.
185. Pitts C.A. General Contractors Ltd.
186. Plastal Manufacturing Ltd.
187. Precision Electronic Components Ltd.
188. Prestolite Company
189. RCA Ltd.
190. Radio Engineering Products Ltd.
191. Raven Industries Ltd.
192. Raytheon Canada Ltd.
193. Renfrew Electric Co. Limited
194. Rochester Iron & Metal Co. Ltd.
195. Scepter Manufacturing Ltd.
196. Scintrex Ltd.
197. Sedeo Systems Inc.
198. Servite International Ltd.
199. Shepherds Auto Supplies Ltd.
200. Sherritt-Gordon Mines Ltd.
201. Singer Valve Co. Ltd.
202. Sinterings Division Bundy of Canada (b)
203. Skil Corp. (Canada) Ltd.
204. Slater Steel Industries Limited
205. Smith David Steel Corp.
206. Societe Industrielle de Decolletage et d'Outillage, Limitee SIDO
207. Sorenson Painters Ltd.
208. Space Research Institute

209. Spar Aerospace Products Ltd.
210. Sperry-Rand Canada Ltd.
211. R. J. Stampings Co. Ltd.
212. Standard-Modern Tool Ltd.
213. Steel Treaters of Quebec
214. Stokes, Hubert Ltd.
215. Summer Tire & Automotive Ltd.
216. Summit Industrial Corp.
217. Supreme Precision Castings Ltd.
218. Systems Research Ltd.
219. TAMCO Limited
220. Thypin Steel Co. Ltd.
221. Transair Ltd.
222. Triad Corp.
223. Triplex Engineering Co. Ltd. TEC
224. Unifin
225. Uniroyal Ltd.
226. United Aircraft of Canada Ltd.
227. United Dairy Equipment Ltd.
228. Universal Die & Tool
229. Valcartier Industries Inc.
230. Varian Associates of Canada Ltd. (VA)
231. Vicom Limited
232. Electronic Craftsmen, Waterloo, Ont.
233. Westhill Industries Ltd.
234. Wheeler Northland Airways Ltd.
235. Whiteplains Electric Supply Corp.
236. W. C. Wood Ltd.
237. Wire Rope Industries Ltd.

Appendix III

Tables showing distribution of funds in the Defence Research Board "University Grants Program."

TABLE 1
GRANTS IN AID OF EXTRAMURAL RESEARCH—1973
Distribution by Universities and Organizations

University or Organization	Number of Grants	Program Level $
Acadia	1	4,000
Alberta	21	110,500
Arctic Institute of North America	1	7,500
British Columbia	42	262,700
Calgary	21	122,300
Carleton	9	42,300
Collège Militaire Royal	11	78,500
Dalhousie	11	33,600
Guelph	10	72,700
Lakehead	3	19,500
Laurentian	1	6,500
Laval	28	171,800
Manitoba	14	70,100
McGill	36	301,250
McMaster	22	123,100
Memorial	6	26,000
Montréal	18	173,700
New Brunswick	12	73,300
Nova Scotia Technical College	3	21,000
Ottawa	14	71,600
Québec	4	23,200
Queen's	19	87,800
Royal Military College	32	309,900
Royal Roads Military College	8	13,250
St. Thomas	1	2,500
Saskatchewan	13	67,000
Saskatchewan (Regina)	3	10,500
Sherbrooke	11	157,900
Sir George Williams	1	4,500

Toronto	53	265,900
Trent	1	5,000
Victoria	5	19,500
Waterloo	34	191,650
Western Ontario	14	97,800
York	14	64,775
GRAND TOTAL	497	3,113,125

TABLE 2

GRANTS IN AID OF EXTRAMURAL RESEARCH—1973

Distribution by Research Areas of Interest to Defence

Research Areas of Interest to Defence	Number of Grants	Program Level $
Military Aspects of Chemical Energy Sources	28	149,500
Electrical Power Sources for Military Applications	25	111,000
Protection Against Chemical Hazards	17	114,800
Metallic and Ceramic Materials Research for Defence Applications	47	391,000
Polymeric and Composite Materials Research for Defence Applications	26	150,500
Military Transportation and Vehicle Engineering	10	57,450
Military Engineering Research	29	172,750
Defence Aspects of Aerodynamic Engineering and Space Technology	29	146,000
Military Radar and Communications Research	55	345,050
Underwater Physics and Engineering	14	96,000
Geotechnical Aspects of Defence Operations	32	180,100
Surveillance Sensor Research	18	157,000
Information Processing Research	47	306,800
Protection Against Radiation Hazards	19	97,000
Military Preventive Medicine	20	107,600
Physiological and Metabolic Stress in Military Environment	19	105,000
Military Visual, Auditory, and Orientation Problems	14	162,800
Air Safety Research	1	5,000

Human Performance and Human Engineering	22	123,275
Defence Aspects of Social Research	5	18,500
Political, Economic, and Strategic Studies for Defence	17	71,000
Institutional Grants	3	45,000
GRAND TOTAL	497	3,113,125

Appendix IV

Pages from the report, "How to Make a Killing," showing details of grants paid by the Pentagon for defence research in Canadian institutions.

U.S. Defense Dept. Grants for *Basic Scientific Research* (Non-Profit Institutions) in Canada

	1967	1968	1969	1970	1971
			[in dollars]		
Univ. of Alberta (Calgary and Edmonton)	69,142	9,890	15,008	X	12,075
Arctic Instit. of North America (Quebec)	38,729	X	X	X	X
British Columbia Research Service	181	851	1,644	X	X
Univ. of British Columbia	9,903	47,135	22,350	X	X
Univ. of Calgary	6,820	X	X	X	X
Canadian Council for Nondestructive Technology (Quebec)	3,000	X	X	X	X
Laval Univ. (Quebec)	15,006	15,006	X	X	X
Univ. of Manitoba (Winnipeg)	X	30,185	X	X	X
McGill Univ. (Montreal)	55,725	24,149	19,896	49,225	19,420
McMaster Univ. (Hamilton)	X	54,784	X	X	X
Univ. of Montreal	X	X	7,300	X	X
Queens Univ. (Kingston)	9,100	12,000	9,933	X	X
Royal Victoria Hospital (Montreal)	X	25,000	X	X	X
Univ. of Saskatchewan (Regina)	X	X	13,717	X	X
Univ. of Toronto	164,778	131,202	101,702	77,027	45,658
Victoria Univ. (Victoria)	X	10,000	10,000	X	X
Waterloo Univ.	32,258	X	X	13,271	35,000
Univ. of Western Ontario (London)	24,553	X	X	X	5,610
Univ. of Windsor	29,941	X	X	X	X
York Univ. (Toronto)	X	X	27,000	X	30,000
TOTAL	459,136	360,202	521,802	139,523	147,763

Five Year Total—4,183,186

Note: The sums include i) outright grants ii) Title to Equipment grants and Title to Equipment contracts.

U.S. Dept. of Defense Grants to Educational and Non-Profit Institutions Receiving Military Prime Contracts of $10,000 or More for Research, Developmental, Test, and Evaluation Work in Canada

	1967	1968	1969	1970	1971
		[in thousands of dollars]			
Univ. of British Columbia	163	135	64	85	83
Canadian Commercial Corporation	X	7,315	5,831	9,026	6,215
Defense Research Board Canadian Joint Staff	X	431	X	X	21
Hospital for Sick Children	18	X	X	X	X
McGill Univ. (Montreal)	212	142	255	32	22
McMaster (Hamilton)	18	X	X	X	X
Univ. of Montreal	74	43	14	X	X
Queens Univ. (Kingston)	X	10	X	X	X
Univ. of Saskatchewan (Regina)	15	12	15	X	X
Univ. of Toronto	99	130	35	20	X
Univ. of Western Ontario (London)	29	30	X	X	X
Univ. of Windsor	X	60	62	X	25
York Univ.	X	26	19	X	X
TOTAL	628	8,334	6,295	9,163	6,366

Five Year Total—30,786,000

From: *Congressional Record* May 1, 1969

Military Dept. Contract Agency	Title	Cost of project (thous.)	Est. date of com-pletion	Contract/ Grant no
	CANADA			
A* York University	Kinetics of Atmospheric Constituents	$52.5	April 1970	DA-AROD-31-124-G868
A McGill University	Extremely Low Frequency Electromagnetic Phenomena	35.8	March 1969	DA-AROD-31-124G1000
A Canadian Commercial Corp.	Meteorological R.D.T. & E. Rocket	296	March 1969	DA-AROI-58-C-0022
A Royal Victoria Hospital	Investigation of Pathogenesis and Treatment of Shock	75	April 1969	PA49-193-G-9248
A University of Manitoba	Study of Factors Influencing the Passage of Drugs into the Malarial Parasite Plasmodium Berghri	20	Feb. 1969	DAPA17-68-G-9257
N McGill University	Electric Properties of Ice	51	March 1969	NONR 4417(00)
N McGill University	Arctic Plankton Ecology	82	April 1969	NCOO14-66-C-0233
N McGill University	HF Audio Absorption in Ice	74	March 1969	NLNR 4915(00)
N McGill University	Energy Budget and Other Tropical Microclimatological Research	19	Feb. 1969	NOCO14-63-C-0307
N Computing Devices of Canada	Automatic Detection and Classification	545	June 1969	N62269-68-C-0291

*Military Department Code: A—Army; N—Navy; F—Air Force; D—ARPA

A	Manitoba University	Investigations of Phoromones as Chemosterilants for Insects with special reference to Synthetic Queen Substance and its Analogues	59.2	Aug. 1969	DADA 17-68-G-9267
N	Institute of Oceanography	Systematics Biology and Hydrographic Relations of Some Species of Oalunus	59	Feb. 1969	NONR4458(00)
N	British Columbia Research Council	Marine Borer Biology	25	March 1969	NONR4505(00)
N	McGill University	Assessment of Military Performance Enhancement by Drugs	139	June 1969	NONR4896(00)
N	York University	Brain Nucleic Acid Changes During Learning	101	Sept. 1969	NONR4935(00)
N	McGill University	Mechanisms of Polymer Degradation	26	May 1970	N00014-68-C 0237
N	McGill University	High Magnetic Fields and Insulators	112	Aug. 1969	NONR 3013(00)
N	Queen's University	Conference on the Structure of Density Matrices and Their Application to energy and Order Effects Problems in matter	10	Feb. 1969	NOOO14-67-C-0388
N	University of Toronto	Very-High Altitude Missile and Decoy Gas Dynamics; Missile Aerodynamics for Broad Altitude Ranges	161	Aug. 1969	NONR4073(00)

Military Dept.	Contract Agency	Title	Cost of project (thous.)		Contract/ Grant no
N	University of British Columbia	Fundamental Air-Sea Exchange Processes and Their Relation to Wind Wave Generation: Oceanic Turbulence	165	Oct. 1969	N00014-66-C 0047
F	University of Western Ontario	Dual-Cavity Microwave Refractometer Study	30	Oct. 1969	F19628-68-C-0128
F	University of Saskatchewan	Conduct Research on the Aurora and Airglow	15	Dec. 1969	F19628-69-C-0106
F	University of Alberta	Lattice Inves. of Critical Phase Transition Temperatures	60	June 1970	AF-AF0SR-1310-67
F	Queens University	Res. Seminar on Reduced Density Matrices	21.1	May 1969	AF-AF0SR-1801-68
F	University of Toronto	Research on Hypervelocity Launchers	294	Aug. 1969	AF-33-615-C5313
F	University of Toronto	Aerodynamically Generated Sound	101.8	Dec. 1969	AF-AF0SR-C672-67A
F	University of Toronto	Symposium on Aerodynamic Noise	4	Oct. 1969	AF-AFOSR-1423-68
F	University of Toronto	Seventh International Shock Tube Symposium	15	Jan. 1970	AF-AFOSR-1550-68
F	University of Toronto	Aerophysical Investigation at Hypervelocities	119.1	March 1970	AF-AFOSR-1388-68
F	University of Toronto	Kinetics of Atomic Associated Reactions Using Flash Photolysis			

		over a Wide Temperature Range	76.2	Oct. 1969	AF-AFOSR-1695-69
F	University of Toronto	Molecular Interactions and Crystal Structures at Low Temperatures	68.7	Jan. 1970	AF-AFOSR-1549-68
F	University of Toronto	Transfer of Mass Momentum and Energy in Free Molecule Systems	129.9	Jan. 1969	AF-AFOSR-1431-68
F	University of Toronto	Plasma Dynamics and Magnetogasdynamics	97.2	Feb. 1969	AF-AFOSR-1290-67
F	McGill University	Formation and Propagation Mechanisms of Diverging Detonation Waves	23	Feb. 1969	AF-AFOSR-1290-67
F	University of Waterloo	Fundamental Processes in Solid Propellant Ignition	32	Feb. 1970	AF-AFOSR-1274-67
F	University of Toronto	Selective Excitation Spectroscopic Diagnostics	33.7	July 1970	AF-AFOSR-1508-68
F	University of Western Ontario	Some Thermochemical Studies by Mass Spectroscopy	34.9	Aug. 1969	AF-AF0SR-1356-68
F	McMaster University	Inorganic Nuclear-Magnetic Resonance Spectroscopy	117.6	March 1970	AF-AFOSR-1567-68
F	University of British Columbia	Chemical Reactions in Frozen Solutions	68.5	Feb. 1970	AF-AFOSR-1102-66A
F	University of Toronto	The Numerical Integration of Ordinary Differential Equations	45.36	Sept. 1960	AF-AFOSR-1357-68
F	University of Toronto	Research on Dynamics of Flight Vehicles	26.1	Dec. 1969	AF-AFOSR-1490-68A

Military Dept. Contract Agency	Title	Cost of project (thous.)	Est. date of completion	Contract/Grant no
F University of British Columbia	Spectral Problems for Elliptic Operators	77.78	May 1969	AF-AFOSR-1531-68
F Canadian Commercial Corp. Washington, D.C.	Ellipsometric Studies of Plasma Anodization	30	Sept. 1969	F33615-68-C-1074
F Canadian Commercial Corp. Washington, D.C.	Research on Excitation Transfer Cross Section	30	May 1969	F33615-68-C-1511
F Canadian Commercial Corp. Washington, D.C.	Correlation of Plasma Analysis Technique	54	Aug. 1969	F33615-68-C-1019
F McGill University	Study of Cloud and Precipitation Physics Utilizing Radar Techniques	0	Nov. 1969	F19628 69-C-0107
F University of Toronto	Infrared Chemiluminescence Studies	40	March 1970	F19628-68-C-0271
F Laval University	Neurohumoral Control of Thyrotrophic Activity	103	Sept. 1969	AF-AFOSR-1627-69
F Barringer Research, Ltd.	Remote Vapor Detection	64	July 1969	AF38(615-63-C-1101)
F Canadian Commercial Corp. Washington, D.C.	Electro-Optic Crystals for Displays	75	July 1969	F30602-63 C-007
D McGill University	Psychological Processes of the Central Nervous System	700.8	June 1971	DAHC15 63-C0396
D University of Windsor	Collisional and Radiation Processes in Atoms and Molecules	66	Aug. 1969	NOOO1467-00538

D	Canadian Armament Research and Development Est.	Hypervelocity Research Program	4,642	Dec. 1969	DA01021AMC-144682
D	RCA Victor Ltd.	Radar Backscatter Studies	195	Nov. 1969	F0469567Co158
D	University of Toronto	Roman Spectra	111.1	May 1969	Nonr 5012 (00)

Appendix V

An extract from the Public Accounts records which give the names of the corporations that received cash grants and allotments in fiscal year 1972-1973 under the Defence Industry Productivity Program (DIP), including a list of grants for fiscal year 1973-1974 to September 30, 1973.

To develop and sustain the technological capability of Canadian defence industry for the purpose of defence export sales arising from that capability
  a) by supporting selected development programs
  b) by paying one-half of the cost of the acquisition of new equipment required for plant modernization and
  c) by supporting the establishment of production capacity and qualified sources for production of component parts and materials on terms and conditions approved by the Treasury Board.

	Estimated	Expenditures
	$	$
Contractors:	162,981,141	
Aero Machine Ltd.— Montreal, Que.		25,000
Aircraft Appliances & Equipment Ltd.— Rexdale, Ont.		69,995
Allis-Chalmers (Rumely) Ltd.—Guelph, Ont.		92,800
Amphenol Canada Ltd.—Scarborough, Ont.		40,500
Atco Industries Ltd.—Calgary, Alta.		183,488
Aviation Electric Ltd.—Montreal, Que.		206,354
Bata Industries Ltd.—Batawa, Ont.		58,812
Bowmar Canada Ltd.—Ottawa, Ont.		371,081
Bristol Aerospace (1968) Ltd.— Winnipeg, Man.		299,960
C A E Electronics Ltd.—Montreal, Que.		1,368,851
C A E Industries Ltd.—Montreal, Que.		22,344
C A E Machinery Ltd.—Vancouver, B.C.		40,879
Canada Superconductor & Cryogenics Co. Ltd.—St. Lambert, Que.		72,500
Canadair Ltd.—Montreal, Que.		5,425,570
Canadian Acme Screw & Gear Ltd.— Toronto, Ont.		54,529

	Estimated	Expenditures
Canadian Aircraft Ltd.—Richmond, B.C.		39,025
Canadian Industries Ltd.—Montreal, Que.		109,990
Canadian Marconi Ltd.—Montreal, Que.		2,913,608
Canadian Steel Foundries Ltd.—Montreal, Que.		99,940
Canadian Timken Ltd.—St. Thomas, Ont.		170,822
Canadian Vickers Ltd.—Montreal, Que.		136,642
Canadian Westinghouse Co. Ltd.—Hamilton, Ont.		41,434
Collins Radio Co. Ltd.—Toronto, Ont.		426,580
Computing Devices of Canada Ltd.—Ottawa, Ont.		472,010
Croven Ltd.—Whitby, Ont.		105,446
Davie Shipbuilding Ltd.—Levis, Que.		72,836
De Havilland Aircraft of Canada Ltd.—Toronto, Ont.		5,938,014
Design Precision Casting Ltd.—Brampton, Ont. (Brook Mfg. Div.)		15,643
Dominion Aluminium Fabricating Ltd.—Toronto, Ont.		39,430
Dominion Forge Co. Ltd.—Windsor, Ont.		37,201
Dominion Road Machinery Co. Ltd.—Goderich, Ont.		21,354
Douglas Aircraft Co. of Canada Ltd.—Toronto, Ont.		2,562,562
Dowty Equipment of Canada Ltd.—Ajax, Ont.		32,500
W. R. Elliott Co. Ltd.—Kitchener, Ont.		73,622
Erie Technological Prod. Ltd.—Trenton, Ont.		162,484
Fathom Oceanology Ltd.—Port Credit, Ont.		171,556
Gabriel of Canada Ltd.—Toronto, Ont.		22,724
Garrett Mfg. Ltd.—Rexdale, Ont.		506,258
General Precision Ind. Ltd.—Montreal, Que.		112,628
Haley Industries Ltd.—Haley, Ont.		24,033
Hammond Mfg. Co. Ltd.—Guelph, Ont.		78,271

	Estimated	Expenditures
John T. Hepburn Ltd.—Toronto, Ont.		51,775
Hermes Electronics Ltd.—Woodside, N.S.		101,223
Heroux Ltd.—Montreal, Que.		51,929
Holland Hitch of Canada Ltd.—Woodstock, Ont.		60,117
Huhn Seal Co. Ltd.—Montreal, Que.		73,030
Husky Mfg. & Tool Works Ltd.—Bolton, Ont.		20,013
I.B.M. Machine Ltd.—Bromont, Que.		553,498
Ingersol Machine & Tool Ltd.—Ingersol, Ont.		3,393
International Parts (Canada) Ltd.—Scarborough, Ont.		5,065
International Tool Ltd.—Windsor, Ont.		31,174
Irvin Industries Ltd.—Fort Erie, Ont.		6,859
K. K. Precision Ltd.—Downsview, Ont.		9,031
Laurentian Concentrates Ltd.—Ottawa, Ont.		13,580
Leigh Instruments Ltd.—Carleton Place, Ont.		318,381
Linamar Machine Ltd.—Ariss, Ont.		74,212
Lister Bolt & Chain Ltd.—Richmond, B.C.		30,800
Litton Systems (Canada) Ltd.—Rexdale, Ont.		2,064,033
Marine Industries Ltd.—Sorel, Que.		801,434
Maritime Industries Ltd.—Vancouver, B.C.		15,650
Marsland Engineering Ltd.—Waterloo, Ont.		505,277
Mega System Design Ltd.—Scarborough, Ont.		43,828
Menasco Mfg. Ltd.—Montreal, Que.		367,536
Microsystems International Ltd.—Ottawa, Ont.		6,071,645
Novatronics of Canada Ltd.—Stratford, Ont.		57,765
Precision Electronics Ltd.—Toronto, Ont.		15,581
Radio Engineering Ltd.—Montreal, Que.		474,300
R.C.A. Ltd.—Montreal, Que.		519,004

	Estimated	Expenditures
Saint John Shipbuilding—St. John, N.B.		89,811
Scepter Mfg. Ltd.—Toronto, Ont.		76,252
C. R. Snelgrove Co. Ltd.—Ottawa, Ont.		148,574
Spar Aerospace Ltd.—Malton, Ont.		192,676
R. J. Stamping Ltd.—Toronto, Ont.		349,614
Standard Prod. (Canada) Ltd.— Stratford, Ont.		3,540
United Aircraft of Canada Ltd.— Longueuil, Que.		11,972,041
H. E. Vannater Ltd.—Wallaceburg, Ont.		134,301
Varian Associates of Canada Ltd.— Georgetown, Ont.		64,140
Velan Engineering Ltd.—Montreal, Que.		169,530
Vestshell Inc.—Montreal, Que.		63,725
Vicom Ltd.—Kingston, Ont.		77
Walbar Machine Prod. Ltd.—Toronto, Ont.		1,102
	162,981,141	48,324,792
Less: Authorized Commitments for subsequent fiscal years	114,651,141	
	$48,330,000	$48,324,792

Defence Industry Productivity Program
Expenditures for Fiscal Year 1973-1974 to September 30, 1973

	Estimated	Expenditures
	$124,509,074	
Bristol Aerospace		$ 153,133
United Aircraft of Canada Ltd.		5,384,955
Canadair Ltd.		2,504,522
Aviation Electric Ltd.		291,308
The de Havilland Aircraft of Canada Ltd.		7,237,717
Fathom Oceanology Ltd.		76,206
Menasco Canada Ltd.		95,847
Garrett Mfg. Ltd.		639,113
Irvin Airchute Ltd.		2,479
Microsystems International Ltd.		2,743,915
Varian Associates of Canada Ltd.		53,598
Erie Technological Products Ltd.		89,935

Canadian Marconi	1,278,588
Computing Devices of Canada Ltd.	80,923
Novatronics of Canada Ltd.	31,491
Mega Systems Design Ltd.	4,738
Radio Engineering Products Ltd.	184,942
C. R. Snelgrove	36,862
Canadian Admiral	9,457
Litton Systems (Canada) Ltd.	753,976
ATCO Industries Ltd.	43,602
St. John Shipbuilding	4,556
Haley Industries Ltd.	36,548
Douglas Aircraft Co. of Canada Ltd.	156,570
Aircraft Appliances	155,155
Canadian Vickers	25,302
Maritime Industries Ltd.	9,909
Marine Industries Ltd.	22,500
Canadian Steel Foundries	16,052
Spar Aerospace Products Ltd.	232,111
W. R. Elliott	31,317
Patenaude	35,500
Arell	16,235
General Metallic Parts	6,159
Huhn Seal	47,841
Canadian Timkin	16,967
Bata Industries	5,487
Bowmar Canada Ltd.	37,227
Westinghouse Canada	$ 1,591
IBM	44,500
Precision Electronics	890
Marsland Engineering	26,178
Croven	16,338
Hammond Mfg.	875
C-Tech	12,686
Allis Chalmers	58,034
Eastern Die	70,711
DBM	32,621
Dominion Road Machinery	243,730
Premier Metal	10,074
Design Precision Castings	53,968

	$124,509,074	$23,495,340
Less—Authorized Commitments for subsequent fiscal years	80,759,035	
	$43,750,039	$23,495,340

Appendix VI

Grants received by Corporations under the Defence Industrial Research Program.

Company	1962-63	1963-64	1964-65	1972-73	1973-74
Abex Industries of Canada Limited	$ 10,789	$ 8,597	$ 17,037	$ 4,319	$ 5,271
Aerovox Canada Limited			3,372	11,110	
Almax Ceremaic Industries Limited				68,873	100,317
Atlas Steels Company Limited	29,620	33,657	15,290	15,000	
Aviation Electric Limited	19,587	16,333	34,941		
Bach-Simpson Limited			24,927		
Bell Northern Research Limited	180,253	228,114	415,988	321,828	56,490
Bowmar Canada Limited			43,895	174,187	201,554
Bristol Aerospace Limited			20,690	92,366	56,831
Clevite Burgess Limited ⌉			8,958		
Canada Superconducting & Cryogenics					25,000
Canada Wire & Cable Limited				30,384	84,617
Canadair Limited	1,766	71,706	137,015	174,423	255,609
Canadian Aviation Electronics Limited	19,676	130,218	80,867	96,876	122.412
Canadian General Electric Company Limited	14,887	90,213	113,213		
Canadian Industries Limited				10,074	
Canadian Marconi Limited			16,444		
Canadian Technical Tape Limited		11,995	27,543		
Canadian Thin Films Limited				83,979	76,121
Canadian Vickers Limited			12,032		

Company	1962-63	1963-64	1964-65	1972-73	1973-74
Canadian Westinghouse Company Limited	$ 33,278	$ 111,984	$ 89,033	$	$
Central Dynamics Limited	7,366	33,000	45,576		
Clevite Burgess Limited		7,682	21,012		
Cominco Limited	18,426	36,097		19,664	93,500
Computing Devices of Canada Limited		101,671	58,305	2,684	
C-Tech Limited				16,758	26,786
CTS of Canada Limited	32,578	133,716	151,404		
DeHaviland Aircraft of Canada Limited	663,174	536,587	641,898	284,756	427,511
Dominion Magnesium Limited	217	1,899	8,152		
Duplate Canada Limited			8,645	151,678	133,000
EDO Canada Limited		27,133	43,755		
EMI Cossor Electronics Limited		25,240	21,016		
Erie Technological Products of Canada Limited		52,356	24,550		
ESE Limited				67,934	16,366
Ferranti Packard Electric Limited	49,853	105,652	164,361	39,005	
Ferrox Iron Limited			97,485		
Fiberglas Canada Limited				78,297	70,000
Fleet Manufacturing Limited				7,670	896
Free Piston Development Limited		83,265	172,438		
Frigistors Limited	932	38,921	95,657		
Garrett Manufacturing of Canada Limited				174,745	161,255

Company	1962-63	1963-64	1964-65	1972-73	1973-74
Gen-Tec Incorporated	$	$	$	$ 93,330	$ 54,936
Geo-Met Reactive Ltd.		28,855	31,745	21,724	
Gould Manufacturing of Canada Limited					
Gulton Industries (Canada) Limited			37,107		
Honeywell Controls Limited		92,543	124,340		
Huntec (70) Limited		1,467	26,755	36,007	11,831
Lignosol Chemicals Limited				16,890	20,441
Litton Systems Canada Limited		1,394	118,521	47,838	38,949
Magnesium Company of Canada Limited			14,994		
Mallory Battery of Canada Limited		6,300	31,560		
Multi-State Devices Limited					
National Semiconductors Limited	14,560	34,389	53,288	348,138	240,000
Nautical Electronic Laboratories Limited				51,710	34,930
Noranda Research Centre			34,149		
Northern Pigment Company Limited				110,579	26,669
Norton Research Corporation (Canada) Limited		10,446	83,876		
Orenda Limited		17,824	21,904	78,740	160,816
Peace River Mining and Smelting Limited			43,597		
Precision Electronic Components Limited				92,344	106,656
RCA Limited	38,103	142,520	171,761	157,176	219,677

Company	1962-63	1963-64	1964-65	1972-73	1973-74
Sherritt Gordon Mines Limited	$ 12,053	$ 100,041	$ 70,483	$ 42,199	$ 62,500
Simiec Industries Limited				89,801	
Sinclair Radio Laboratories Limited				76,667	31,924
Spar Aerospace Products Limited				184,567	
Sperry Gyroscope of Canada Limited		40,932	3,437		
Sprague Electric of Canada Limited			11,849		
Techwest Enterprises Limited				77,835	85,915
Unican Security Systems Limited				26,376	83,742
United Aircraft of Canada Limited	37,326	194,326	272,345	678,067	730,626
Varian Associates of Canada Limited	13,380	18,192	21,775	47,244	
Welwyn Canada Limited		7,460	50,283		33,250
GRAND TOTALS	$1,197,824	$2,582,725	$3,839,268	$4,203,842	$3,856,398

Appendix VII

For the fiscal year 1973-1974, the Defence Research Board has been allocated cash estimates of $50,894,000: of this amount, $41,431,000 represents operating expenditures, $7,500,000 is provided for contributions to industry and universities, and $1,963,000 covers statutory contributions to the superannuation account.

Diagram 1 shows the percentage distribution of funds by activity and Diagram 2 shows the percentage distribution of funds by establishments.

Diagram 1

Percentage Distribution of Funds by Activity—1973-1974

Program Activity

1. Laboratory Applied Research	52.5%
2. Analytical Support for Defence	6.0%
3. Defence Scientific Liaison & Information Services	3.7%
4. Stimulation and Support of Defence Research	15.8%
5. Administration and Site Services	18.1%
6. Civilian Pension Contributions	3.9%

Diagram 2

Percentage Distribution of Funds by Establishment—1973-1974

Defence Research Establishment Atlantic	9.4%
Defence Research Establishment Valcartier	24.8%
Defence Research Analysis Establishment	4.6%
Defence Research Establishment Ottawa	13.8%
Defence and Civil Institute of Environmental Medicine	5.3%
Defence Research Establishment Suffield	6.9%
Defence Research Establishment Pacific	6.5%
Headquarters—Central Administration	12.0%
Defence Industrial Research Program	9.4%
University Grants Program	7.3%

Index

A

Abu Dhabi 57
Air Defence Command 75
Air Force Office of Scientific Research 85
Algeria 47
Allen, Dudley 56
Anaconda Copper Mining Company 31-32, 101
Annual Report of the Department of Trade and Commerce (1968) 30
Argentina 10, 53
Arms export 1, 3, 5-6, 8-10, 16-19, 24-25, 27-28, 30-31, 34, 39-59
Arms merchants 1-3, 18-19, 34-62
Assured supply 18-20
Australia 53, 57, 73
A. V. Roe Canada, Ltd. 22
Avro *Arrow* 22-24

B

Balance of power 2, 10
Balance of trade 44
Barter system 17-20
Belgium 53
Bell Aerospace Canada 98
Board of Transport Communications 32
Botsawana 10, 53
Brazil 10, 30, 53
Broadbent, Ed 69, 83
Brunei 53
Burma 53
Buy America Act 7, 25, 44

C

Cadieux, Leo 83-84
Cameroons 57
Canada-United States Defence Development and Production Sharing Program 25-30
Canadair Ltd. 57, 61, 89, 94-95, 101, 118, 121, 123
Canadian Armed Forces 13, 23, 53-57, 71, 79, 91, 96, 99-100
Canadian Arsenals 50
Canadian Commercial Corporation 18, 36-37, 53, 84, 87, 112
Canadian Defence Products 37, 56, 57, 94-100
Canadian Development Corporation 61
Canadian Industries Ltd. 52, 102, 119